A Woman's Guide
to *Revenge*

S0-ABB-217

A Woman's Guide to *Revenge*

Greg and Ann Clouthier

Private Investigators

SelectBooks, Inc.

A Woman's Guide to Revenge

Copyright ©2005 Greg and Ann Clouthier.

This edition published by SelectBooks, Inc. For information, address SelectBooks, Inc., New York, NY 10003.

Cover photograph by Jonathan Scott Walnut Creek, CA

All rights reserved. Published in the United States of America. No part of this book may be used or reproduced in any manner whatsoever without the written permission of the publisher.

First Edition

ISBN 1-59079-071-5

Library of Congress Cataloging-in-Publication Data

Clouthier, Greg, 1947–
A woman's guide to revenge / by Greg and Ann Clouthier.
    p. cm.
ISBN 1-59079-071-5 (pbk. : alk. paper)
1. Adultery. 2. Women–Psychology. 3. Revenge. I. Clouthier, Ann. II. Title.
HQ806.C56 2005
306.73'6'09794–dc22

                              2005003753

Manufactured in the United States of America

10 9 8 7 6 5 4 3 2 1

Contents

Dedication

This book is dedicated to the women in my life, starting with the two most important: my wife, coauthor, and best friend, Ann; and my mother, Grace. Both allowed me to question them about matters of the heart and generously shared their wisdom. I appreciate their faithfulness.

The other women in my life are those who permitted me to help them bring some closure to their betrayed lives. They are all wonderful beings who I consider to be my friends.

A special thanks is also given to friends and family who encouraged me to write these stories. They enjoyed hearing them and assured me they would make for good reading. I am especially grateful to:

- Richard Pearlman, my good friend who spent many hours devoting his input to this project;
- R.W. Lynch, for encouragement and friendship;
- Linda Catron, for providing a sanctuary for this author to write this book;
- To Don Nienhouse, now one of God's angels, faithful husband to his wife Marilee and my best friend.

Introduction

It's very important to understand that infidelity has been going on for thousands of years and the investigative tools of the trade have advanced as well as become obsolete during that same period. Our laws were very liberal during the past fifty years; however as technology has advanced, our laws have changed, making eavesdropping, bugging, and wiretapping illegal. During the 1990s laws were adopted to stop the recording of, or listening to, wireless communications over the air. With the advancement of the Internet and computer use, new laws will stop the monitoring of e-mails from off-site computers. What I'm saying is that while it's getting easier and easier to get away with cheating and lying, there are always ways around some of the laws for monitoring communications between two unsuspecting parties. Because these stories date back from the 1970s to the present day, terms used such as "bugging" the phone, etc., are easier to use rather than going into a more technical description. It is also important to know that the laws that govern Americans, govern Americans here in the U.S.A. Many foreign countries have very liberal laws about monitoring the spoken word. So if your husband is planning on taking his grope south of the border, you may be able to receive video

... with audio. And how has technology helped us? Thanks to GPS (Global Positioning Satellite), we can plant a tiny device and follow him anywhere on earth. GOTCHA!

My wife, Ann, is one of the most beautiful women I have ever met. I fell madly in love with her the moment I saw her. If you were to meet Ann, you would never guess that she was a private investigator. She has an air of serenity and gentleness about her. I, on the other hand, look more the part of a private investigator. In my younger days I would have described myself as having more of a Robert Wagner persona, but these days I'd have to say I could pass for Jack Nicholson's brother.

Ann loves to write, and I can hold my own as a storyteller. After years of hearing folks say, "You should write a book about your experiences," we collaborated to do just that. This book is intended to not only share what we've learned about infidelity, but also share what we've learned about how absolutely clever woman are when dealing with matters of the heart. We do not wish to trivialize the painful experiences our clients have had to endure. Rather, these stories reveal how women have stepped up to the very emotional challenge with purpose and poise. We would never recommend that a woman seek revenge on their partner; to do so could be very dangerous. If nothing more were to be said, we've learned that the feminine mind, when provoked, can be utterly determined and creative in arriving at a strategy and seeing the plan through to "get even." These 23 true stories are an easy read that will have you commiserating and laughing aloud; all the while educating you on the symptoms of infidelity.

Nearly twenty-five years ago I opened my first office in the San Francisco Bay Area suburb of Lafayette, California. Ann, at the time, worked as a legal secretary in a family law office, and most of my earliest clients were referrals from that law firm. I'll always remember my first client, Cindy, a willowy blonde in her mid thirties. She refused the offer of a cup of coffee, and I could immediately sense the anxiety in her body movement and speech. She sat down across from my desk, nervously opened a manila folder, and presented me with a photograph of her soon-to-be ex-husband, Michael.

"That's him. I believe he's cheating on me. We've been married more than 16 years and now it has come to this."

I glanced down at the photograph to see a smiling, very corporate looking forty-year-old man with salt and pepper hair. "What makes you think he's having an affair," I asked her.

Cindy stated that, as long as she had known Michael, he's worn white J.C. Penny's Towncraft boxers. But he'd recently decided to wear colored bikini style underwear.

"Any other symptoms of infidelity?" I asked.

After pondering for a moment, Cindy replied, "It was always me who pushed him away from sexual advances, but now he seems to be too tired. Ever since he turned forty, he's been worried about his hairline and personal hygiene." Cindy asked me if she might be over reacting, and I assured her that I have found that most women are very intuitive; if you feel he's up to something ... he probably is. I made notes about her suspicions and decided right then and there to compile a list, to be entitled, "Symptoms of Infidelity." What I didn't realize at the time was Cindy was giving me three of the most common signs: your man turns forty, he's stepped up on his personal hygiene, and his wardrobe changes.

During that first year in practice, I heard nearly every sign of infidelity one could have imagined. Over the past twenty-five years, I've learned one sign that hasn't been repeated. A very gruff and miserable woman in her early fifty's claimed that her husband *must* be having an affair. I asked her "the question," and the reply was as follows: "My husband is a slob. He comes home from work and removes his clothing and sits in his underwear, belching and passing gas in front of the TV, and demands only one thing ... beer. He never remembers my birthday or anniversary. He doesn't know I exist. From the time we were married, he has been a miserable slob. But lately, he is getting dressed up and coming home with flowers for me. I just know that bastard is having an affair. Why would he all of a sudden be so nice?"

"Do you really want the old slob back?" It was difficult for me not to laugh, and I reminded myself that this woman deserved compassion for what she had been going through. I would guess his behavior would come under the category of "a drastic change in personality." But "being nicer" was definitely a new subcategory.

I believe that most of us have experienced the moment when we confront our feeling that our partner is cheating. We think we might be over reacting ... a little or a lot ... and it's not unusual for your partner to try to convince you that it's all in your head and that you're certifiably crazy. It doesn't take long before you think he's right.

Ann and I learned not only about the signs of infidelity but also about the unique and common reactions these women experienced. They generously shared their fears, pain, and especially their sense of humor and strength through their ordeal. We thank them wholeheartedly. Of course, in order to protect their privacy, their true names are not revealed.

Within each story there is a lesson to learn. One of the biggest lessons is that men who cheat will most likely get caught. Men cheat for sport. For a woman to cheat, it's more personal. Women are most competitive with other women. A

wife will inevitably be tipped off to the extramarital relationship by "the other woman." A man would never wish to tip
off a husband! That would bring nothing but agonizing physical pain. Why ruin a good thing? And this brings us to the
next book in the works, *HOTELS ... MOTELS ... BACK-
SEATS ... AND MORE,* which is devoted to the stories of the
cheating woman. For every cheating man, there is probably
a cheating woman. The biggest difference between men and
woman when they learn that their beloved is having an affair
is how they react. Men do exactly that—they REACT!
Women think. They plan with conviction, and they deserve
an Oscar! Women are at their best when it comes to acting
like nothing is happening, whereas a man can't control his
anger when he knows of the other man. I often wondered
how a woman manages to continue with her daily routine,
sleep with him, for months, without divulging that she
knows. I have yet to meet a man who could do that. The spirit of Mata Hari is very much a part of the feminine mystique.

1

A Single
Red Rose

When spring comes to the San Francisco Bay Area, the footprint of fog has long disappeared. Either the rain is falling, or it's a beautiful day and photographers are snapping those crisp, picture-perfect photos you see on souvenir postcards. For many living out West, March is a time to wear short-sleeved shirts and pick up a few rays. It's difficult for us to imagine what it's like to shovel snow and warm the car before the morning's commute. I don't see how those East Coast private eyes can do it.

It had been four hours since Roger had disappeared into the building across the street. I drummed my fingers impatiently on the steering wheel. Peering up through the windshield, I could see the sun still hanging fairly high in a bright, blue sky above the San Francisco Bay. Yawning, I checked my watch: 4:30 p.m.

"C'mon, Roger. I'm getting tired. You didn't even take a lunch break!"

I squirmed in my seat, rubbed my eyes with both fists, pushed the sleeves of my tan cotton sweater farther up my arms, scratched the back of my neck, ran a hand through my hair, and tugged at my ear. As a six-foot-two, 200-pound guy, I was beginning to feel a little antsy. Being wedged under a steering wheel for four hours was causing my underwear to compress and crawl up my ass like a thong bathing suit. For a guy, that's totally unnerving. I lifted my butt off the seat, grabbed at my crotch, and tried to readjust things a little. Not easy when you're wearing jeans, but it helped some. I settled back down to wait some more.

Twenty minutes later, just when I was ready to give up and bail, the sun glinted on an opening door across the street. It was Roger. Trim and athletic, wearing one of those $800 suits and groomed like executives always are, he stepped into the sunlight and headed for his forest green Jag parked in the reserved spot labeled "President."

I sat up straighter, powered up my onboard computer, lifted the antenna, and started the engine. Gripping the steering wheel, I was prepared to follow as soon as the Jag hit the street. My adrenaline was up, nerves at the ready.

"Now ... what the fuck?"

Roger had decided to put the convertible top down on the Jag and was fussing around with it, making sure everything folded into the recess. "C'mon ... move it!" I silently urged. More minutes passed while he struggled with the ragtop. Obviously, my suspect was no mechanical genius.

Finally he got in, started up, and pulled out of his parking space. We were off and running. Less than a minute after we checked onto the freeway, my phone scanner was picking up a call to his latest grope. It was the fourth call I'd covered between them in a week. This time it only rang twice before she answered and I heard the breathy voice whisper, "Hello?"

"Hi, Bunny. Miss me?"

"Yeah, always. You know that, Thumper. Where are you?"

"On the freeway. God, you sound good."

"So do you. You coming by my place?"

"Nah. Can't tonight. Got to get on home to the bitch, make her feel wanted."

"That's OK, 'cause you're all mine this weekend. Make up whatever excuses you have to. Oh, by the way, I made hotel reservations for us for the Bay to Breakers in May."

For those of you who may not know about the Bay to Breakers, it is an open invitation to the public, individually or in groups, in costume or not, to run together through the streets of San Francisco, beginning at the San Francisco Bay and ending at the Pacific Ocean.

After a moment of silence, Roger replied, "Sounds great, Hon. I'll figure something out. How'd you pay for it?"

"The American Express card you gave me, silly. What else?"

"Okay. Good. How much?"

"$340 a night. Two nights. Not bad, huh?"

"Damn, Bunny. Couldn't you find something a little cheaper?"

I could almost hear Bunny's pout over the airwaves.

"Well, you told me ..."

"Yeah, I know. But Donna's been acting suspicious lately. I just don't want that card to come back and bite me in the ass."

I chuckled and thought to myself, "Forget it, Roger old buddy. Your ass is hanging out real bare right now, and

Donna's pit bull is after it, jaws wide open for a solid chomp."

Bunny came right back at him. She knew how to twist Thumper's tail. "Well then, I guess I'll just have to make you forget all about Donna and that silly old hotel bill, won't I? Purrrrrr ..."

He went for it like a pimply-faced teenager in heat. "Can't wait, Bunny. You're making me horny as hell already. Call you tomorrow, okay?"

"Okay." Then she made kissing sounds and whispered, "Keep thinking about what I'm going to do to you on Friday."

They hung up. I slid off the freeway at the next exit and called my client, Donna, to tell her Roger was on his way home. "We've got him this time. Be cool, but be nice, okay? Meet me in an hour at the Brass Door in San Ramon and we'll talk."

I knew his little weekend tryst in May would be the trap my client needed to slam the matrimonial door on her peckerhead of a husband. It wasn't the first time we'd caught ol' Roger with his zipper down. We'd gotten him *en flagrante* twice before, but Donna suffers from what shrinks call the "addicted to love" syndrome.

Not that Roger didn't know Donna like a well-worn book. The bastard knew just how to play her. He had these asinine excuses that any fool could see through like a picture window in a Holiday Homes Development. Any fool, that is, except poor Donna. She wanted so badly to believe that Roger loved her, that they had a solid marriage, that he was a devoted father to their fourteen-year-old daughter and, above all, that he wasn't a skirt-chaser. Roger always convinced Donna that he was an innocent bystander, that she was the wrongful accuser, and that whatever he was doing was for her sake and Jennifer's.

As planned, Donna met me in San Ramon; and while trying to hold back her tears, she listened to the recorded telephone conversation. Then we discussed "The Plan."

Since it was only March, we still had a couple of months to
set things in motion. I informed Donna we didn't need to
spend any more money or time tailing Roger. We'd just wait
until the weekend of the race. Donna's job would be to keep
cool and not show any signs of stress or outward hostilities
towards Roger. You can imagine that this task is much easier
said than done. I told her to tell Roger in late April that she
planned to visit her sister in Tahoe on the weekend of the
Bay to Breakers.

Her immediate task was to contact the hotel where Roger
and Carol had a reservation and reserve two rooms, with one
of them being adjacent to theirs. I told her to tell the reservations clerk that she was going to surprise her best friend
with a birthday party. The clerk bought the story and set her
up in an adjoining room.

The months seemed to drag until May. The calls from Donna to
my office came more and more frequently. We were all nervous
and excited at the same time. I just hoped that Donna wouldn't
lose her composure and attack Roger in the hotel room.

D-Day arrived. It was a warm Saturday morning and Donna
decided to go for a walk in the hills surrounding their home
in the small, upscale town of Danville. She wanted to think
about the day ahead of her and do some soul searching.
When she returned home, she was psyched up and ready to
go. Donna carefully packed Roger's underwear like she
always did, tightly folded and rolled up along with his

Speedos and running shoes, and the dumpy old blue hat he loved to wear while running.

When Donna was done, all of Roger's clothes were neatly folded and placed in his overnight bag. A suit was laid out for him to wear if he decided to go out to dinner. Donna later told me she had selected the suit as if it were the one she would have him buried in. Donna had stopped at her attorney's office a few days earlier and a Petition for Dissolution of Marriage had been filed with the court.

That evening, after Roger had left for San Francisco, I met Donna in Walnut Creek and drove her to the hotel. She and my wife, Ann, were booked in a room on another floor. The plan was for Donna and Ann to have a "girls' night out" before the emotionally packed Sunday.

As we drove, Donna told me how beneficial the earlier walk had been for her. She said she had reflected on the day she told Roger of her Tahoe plans.

"You should have seen his face when I mentioned to him I wanted to take off to Tahoe for the weekend of the Bay to Breakers race. He barely concealed his delight and was obviously trying to hold back tears of joy. I knew he had been planning on asking me to go with him. Of course, if I had agreed to join him, he would have had a built-in negative response. Something like, 'Oh great, Hon! You, I, and the guys will have a wonderful time in the city.' He knew I hated going on these little bullshit trips of his, but he always asked me along as a diversion."

The race was still under way when Bert, another investigator arrived with me at the hotel the next morning. I had asked Bert to join us because I wanted someone big and strong to be with Donna if she lost control during any of the upcoming events.

We all gathered in the room adjacent to the room where Roger and Carol were staying. Ann told us she had been successful in placing the bug behind their bed the day before. We had placed a speaker on the top of our TV with the volume turned down to medium. It was around midday when we heard the two lovers returning from the race.

It took Roger just long enough to pull down his Speedos and for Carol to pull down her panties before the bed began to squeak. The next sounds we heard were your basic "you're so beautiful, oh baby, oh baby! Don't stop! Don't stop! Harder! Harder!" I really thought Donna was going to bolt out and burst into the adjoining room, but she didn't. She just sat quietly waiting to see what he would say next to his lover, who Donna had nicknamed "the Slut." That came a few moments after the climax.

"I love you, Baby."

Then we heard the sound of Roger's dismount, a squeak, and then a thud. Roger drew a breath. "I can't keep going on like this without you. This sneaking away for a few minutes with you is not enough."

Carol asked in her soft, husky voice, "Have you told her yet?"

"It's hard, Baby, it's so hard. As soon as Jennifer graduates from high school, I'll be able to ditch Donna."

"I know you don't want to spend all that money on support payments, but I'd be willing to help, if you let me."

Roger's reply was, "Oh Baby." Then the sound of lips and wet skin rubbing together filled the room as they began their lovemaking again.

After another 35 minutes there was silence. Then we heard a loud squeak and a thud as Roger dismounted and rolled over to his side of the bed. After a few short moments of silence, we heard an unmistakable Farrrrrrrrrrrrrrrt sound. Then another moment of silence until Carol whispered, "Excuse me."

I felt my shoulders begin to shake uncontrollably. My eyes were fixed on the floor. Looking at anyone in the room would have been certain doom. I knew I wasn't the only one. I could see Donna and Ann from the corner of my eye. Each face was buried in a pillow, and they were about to slide off the bed with uncontrollable laughter. Bert made a sound similar to a moose in heat and quickly escaped to the bathroom so he could stifle his laughter with a towel.

Finally, when I couldn't stand it any longer, I got up and left the room. After about fifteen minutes I was finally back in control, so I returned to the room. Donna and Ann were sitting on the beds, not looking at each other for fear of generating mass hysteria. Their eyes were red and puffy. I finally asked, "How's everyone doing?"

"I think the fart broke the ice for us," replied Ann. "It was pretty intense."

"Wait! Hold on!" I whispered. I heard Carol coming out of the shower and Roger going in. "I think we better get prepared to move soon."

By the time Roger got out of the shower, it was still early. Neither Roger nor Carol wanted to go anywhere, so they decided to eat in. This was actually very good because it gave Donna the opportunity to hear them talk about their plans for the future.

Ann and I decided to eat at the restaurant downstairs. Donna didn't want to miss a single word, and asked if we could bring a deli sandwich back for her and Bert.

Roger and Carol talked late into the night, discussing divorce and financial matters. Roger complained of jock itch from the run that morning. As we listened, we heard the familiar statement: "I'll marry you when my daughter graduates from high school." Other popular phrases come to mind, such as: "When my wife goes back to school ... has that needed operation ... or dies." The honest response from Roger should have been, "Carol, just be in my bed until you get older and then I'll trade you in on a younger model."

And how about Donna? Would he divorce her? Nope! He doesn't want to divorce Donna. Not good ol' trusting Donna. After all, she's the mother of his daughter. And what a good little wife she is to look the other way when other women are trying to snare him.

Finally, Donna and Ann returned to their room on the upper floor. Bert and I slept in the room adjoining Roger and Carol's.

Monday morning rolled around. Donna and Ann joined us. At about 9:30 we heard our first conversation.

"Hey Baby ... you awake?"

Carol's reply was a moan. "Roger, not now. It's too early." Roger promised to be gentle, but Carol wasn't interested. "I'm sore! I have your rash all over my tush."

Dr. Roger offered to put some jelly on it and make it feel better. More moans from Carol, soon enough leading to squeak, squeak, squeak.

"Baby, you're so tight, you feel like a teenager."

More groans from Carol.

"Oh yes, oh Baby, ooh ... ooh ... oh yes."

The "oohs" and "ahhs" and balling continued for another twenty minutes, followed by purring and moaning as Carol and Roger collapsed in each other's arms. Again we heard the familiar sound of Roger's dismount, a squeak, and then a thud.

Total silence!

Donna, Bert, Ann and I glanced at one another, waiting. It was too quiet! Would there be a repeat of yesterday's closing sound effects? The anticipation was excruciating. My shoulders started shaking, and so did Bert's. Donna and Ann grabbed their respective pillows, just in case!

I wondered if Roger and Carol were snoozing or just taking a breather before starting up again. Finally, Carol broke the silence.

"Honey, this rash is really bad. It's spreading all over the back of your legs. We'd better put something on you before it spreads any further. I have it all over my tush and under my arms, too. We need to get something for this."

Roger replied that it wasn't uncommon to get a rash after running all morning in the heat, and that they could pick something up while they spent the day sightseeing.

Burt and I followed the loving couple most of the day while Ann and Donna shopped. During the day's activities we videotaped Roger and Carol acting like lovers, holding hands, and exchanging an occasional kiss on the lips.

It was 7:30 in the evening when they returned to the hotel. We knew that Roger had made dinner reservations at the Carnelian Room at the top of the Bank of America Building on California Street for 8:30 p.m. That gave them almost an hour to get dressed.

As soon as they entered the room, Roger started to grope Carol, but she didn't give in to his advances. Personally, I don't think Roger wanted it anymore than she did. I think he just pretended to want sex three times a day to make Carol think he's youthful with an insatiable appetite. Carol's rejection and Roger's acceptance confirmed my suspicions.

While Roger and Carol were getting ready, Ann and I took a cab to the Carnelian Room. Upon arrival we told the maitre d' we needed two separate tables, each for a party of two. The table we chose had a wide view of the dining area. The other was in a corner but also had a good view of the room.

At 8:40 we watched Roger and Carol enter the dining area. They were seated at a table with a spectacular view of the city. Shortly thereafter Donna and Bert arrived. They were escorted to the previously arranged table in the corner. They had a clear view of Roger and Carol. We had an excellent view of both couples.

Ann walked over to Donna and handed her a long white box tied with a large red ribbon and bow. Donna took the box and slipped into the powder room down the hall. She returned a few minutes later, smiling. As she handed the box back to Ann, she whispered that she had put another surprise in the box for Roger. Donna returned to her seat next to Bert.

I turned the video recorder I had brought towards Roger and Carol. I had a clear shot of them smiling and drinking wine, as though they didn't have a care in the world. The plan was for Donna to drop her napkin when she wanted Ann to deliver the box.

We all ate a delicious dinner and timed it so we finished at the same time as Roger and Carol. Donna dropped her napkin. Ann rose from the table, walked across the floor to Roger and Carol's table, handed Roger the long white box with the red ribbon and said, "This is for you."

Roger looked surprised, but Ann didn't say another word. She just turned around and walked out of the main dining room. Roger, clearly perplexed, opened the box. By this time Ann had returned to our table from another direction.

Inside the white box was a single, long-stemmed red rose. Carefully wrapped around it was the petition for divorce. And the little extra surprise gift that Donna had included? It was a small bottle of calamine lotion for Roger's "heat rash," which, in reality, was a rash from poison oak. Donna had carefully rubbed the poison oak leaves across the crotch of Roger's underwear while she was packing for him.

Roger's face turned pale. There was a look of sheer panic as his eyes scanned the restaurant. He froze and visibly gulped as his eyes locked with the all-too-familiar pair of deep blue eyes that were staring back at him. His wife looked beautiful in her sexy evening gown, with her hair all made up and wearing just the right amount of makeup. His eyes then moved towards Bert, who is tall and movie-star handsome. Donna took full advantage of the moment and gave Burt a gentle kiss on the cheek. Then they both stood up and left the restaurant, hand-in-hand. *Touché!*

Why did Roger cheat? First, he had the time and means to. Secondly, he had reached a personal pinnacle of success and felt he had earned it. Plus, his power and success made him more desirable among the younger generation of husband hunters. And finally, he was nice looking, drove a luxury car, and lived in an exquisite home in the gated community of the local country club. What else could a woman want? Single or married, Roger was definitely a catch. Roger was also over forty years old, which is the age when many men feel insecure about their appearance and sexual abilities. Some women, however, gladly accept a man who is poor in the face and physique, if he's rich in the pockets. Ever wonder why some women wear those sleeping masks?

2

Where the Action Is!

Most rendezvous take place in an inexpensive local motel, the back seat of a car, or occasionally in a private home. Dan, the big-time cheater in this story, entertained his fantasies and girlfriends in style.

Dan is in his early fifties, distinguished and successful. Paula, his wife, is an attractive petite blonde with a trim figure and endearing personality. They met while they were in college at Northwestern. Dan was the typical fraternity brother and athlete, quite handsome with an excellent grade point average—despite excessive drinking and womanizing.

Why did Paula knowingly marry a womanizer? For one reason, she was head over heels in love with Dan. And like so many other women in this world, she was sure that marriage would keep Dan's roving eye focused on her and her alone.

My wife, Ann, and I met with Paula at her residence in Torrey Pines, a breathtakingly beautiful seaside resort town

13

just north of San Diego. After talking with Paula, it was obvious that Dan was the classic philanderer and Paula was the classic victim. She couldn't understand how her wonderful husband of twenty years could be having an affair with another woman. Although suspicious that he had bedded other women during their marriage, she refused to accept the telltale signs of a cheating husband. This time, however, she couldn't look away. Things were different and she was afraid this newest interest might be somewhat of a permanent fixture, which is why she had contacted us. She wanted to be absolutely 100% positive that her suspicions were correct.

Dan made a lot of money and Paula was living the lifestyle we would all like to become accustomed to. They had a beautiful home, his and her Mercedes, golf cart, and a top spot on the Social Register. The only thing lacking was their love life. But Paula wrote that off to Dan's devotion to his prosperous business ventures, which included an extraordinary amount of travel without Paula.

"Paula, what are you going to do if Dan is cheating on you?" Ann asked.

Paula looked perplexed. "Well, I guess I would have to divorce him, wouldn't I?"

"Not necessarily," I responded. "This is when Ann Landers (or was it Dear Abby?) says you should ask yourself THE question: Am I better off with him or without him?"

I knew Paula had to weigh her feelings about Dan. She had to decide if she loved him, despite his faults. Could she overlook his philandering, especially in view of the lifestyle he had provided for her? This probably sounds callous and shallow on the surface, but these are very real questions every spouse who is contemplating the end of a marriage must consider.

I looked directly into Paula's eyes as I asked, "Let's say we catch him. What can you do to maintain leverage over his balding head to make sure he'll go limp just thinking about the assets he'll lose if you find out he's cheating?"

"I do love him," Paula said softly, "and I don't know how to make a decision like this."

I reassured Paula she was not alone. In fact, I told her, she'd probably be amazed at how many of her friends were also living with philandering husbands. Remember, Paula lived in a world of financially successful men whose money and power made them desirable, despite their balding heads and bulging tummies.

Paula looked towards my wife and asked what she would do if she caught her husband cheating. Ann glared at me with her big brown Lorena Bobbett eyes and said, "I'd become a widow."

That's one thing about my Annie; I always know exactly where I stand! I also sleep on my stomach!

"Honestly, Paula, I would catch him first and find out a little about his paramour. Is she a gold digger? Married? Is she a quick romp or a serious contender? If he were seeing your best friend, then you'd probably want his and her head on a platter. It's best to find out who it is and then you can deal with the choices."

Paula agreed and retained us to catch her husband. Now it was our job to determine once and for all who Dan was seeing, put the facts on the table (or, more appropriately, on the VCR), and then help Paula to look at her options. The decision to dump Dan had to be wholly hers.

Paula told us that Dan would be picking up his new yacht in about a week. It was berthed in Florida, and he was planning to sail it through the Panama Canal and up the Mexican Riviera to San Diego. The yacht's name was "The Rover," but

Paula showed us a brochure showing that its name had originally been "The Rendezvous." I couldn't help but wonder why he changed it. It was a 120-foot long cabin cruiser with two Chrysler engines. All of us felt that if Dan were cheating on Paula, he would certainly do it on his new yacht. Paula provided us with Dan's itinerary, which allowed us to make our plans. We knew he would have to stop for fuel and supplies, so we plotted a map for likely stopovers.

We asked Paula if she had any idea who Dan was seeing. She said he had offices throughout North America, but had been spending more time than usual at one located in Dade County, Florida. She had wondered why, but what tipped her off that something was going on was her discovery of a credit card receipt for flowers delivered to an employee at the Florida office. Finding that really opened her eyes. She also recalled how Dan had always come home from Florida feeling totally regenerated. She said he never looked so good as when he returned from his Florida trips.

Ann and I felt this surveillance would be easier than some, yet harder than others. Who can miss a 120-foot yacht? It can only be parked in a very limited number of marinas large enough to accommodate such a vessel. But we also knew the only time we could get film of our twosome fondling one another would be when they were on deck or on shore. In that respect, it was going to take some "strategizing."

We made flight arrangements on the red-eye from San Francisco to Florida, and arrived in Miami at 8:00 a.m. We rented a sporty convertible (better to videotape out of) and drove directly over to Dan's corporate offices. We entered the six-story building, hoping to see Dan and perhaps his lady friend. Dan's secretary informed us that her boss was out of town for an extended period of time.

Next stop was the marina. We enjoyed shrimp salads at the local seafood restaurant before taking a walk to find "The Rover." The harbormaster knew about the yacht, and that it had been sold to a fellow on the West Coast. He also knew it had set sail early that morning with the new owner and crew.

We planned to meet the ship at its next docking in Panama City, but considering sailing time and weather conditions, we knew Dan would be at sea for several days. Using her faultless sense of reasoning, Ann convinced me we would have time to visit Disney World. Even though I wanted to tell her to put her mouse ears back in the suitcase, her logic was right on. We went off the clock and enjoyed three days and nights at Disney World. We then flew back to Miami and visited some friends before flying to Panama City the following week.

Upon our arrival in Panama we checked with José, our advance guy. José was an ex-cop and military man who enjoyed the relaxed atmosphere on the equator. His fees were reasonable and he had the manpower to get the job done. He had ordered his men to keep an eye out for "The Rover" and to observe its passengers when it arrived.

Ann and I had reserved rooms at the Hilton, so we went there to begin our wait. José called us the second day to tell us "The Rover" had arrived. We dressed in Panama whites and went directly to the marina. I felt like I was cast in some Bogey movie. The heat was unbearable and I could almost feel the pounds melting off me, but Ann seemed to thrive in the humidity.

We spotted "The Rover," but didn't see anyone on board except a deckhand. I asked where the captain was, and found that he'd also managed to get a room at the Hilton.

Ann and I hailed a cab back to the hotel. Hotel security, as most anything south of the U.S. border, can be bought off fairly inexpensively. Tourists learn this quickly and always keep a few bribery pesos in their pockets. I asked the clerk at the front desk for Mr. Sprickel's room. The clerk handed me the keys!

"Oh you must have misunderstood me," I said, handing the keys back to him. "I just wanted his room number so I can call him." (Of course, I memorized the room number from the key, but the clerk told me the room number anyway.)

Ann and I returned to our room to freshen up and prepare ourselves for an evening of surveillance. We put on our comfortable shoes, gathered plenty of pesos, cameras, and film ... and got ready for action!

Ann placed a call to the room and a male voice answered. "Hello?"

"Is this Dave?"

"No, you have the wrong number."

Ann smiled as she looked at me with that "got 'em" look. "He answered," she said.

We took the elevator up to the 3rd floor, and then quickly and quietly walked to his room. I placed my ear against the door and heard a male voice say, "Let's go."

I quickly jumped back and put my arm around Ann as we casually sauntered towards the elevator. We heard the door open and a couple talking. We slowed down so they could catch up. I held the elevator door for Ann and backed up so the couple behind us could get in. To my amazement, it was not Dan!

"Hi, are you Americans?" I asked.

"Yes," answered the unidentified male. "I'm Doug Armstrong and this is my wife, Carol."

I put my hand out to shake his and introduced myself as Mike Castle and my wife, Sandy.

"What brings you to Panama City," I asked.

Carol piped up, "My husband is a captain of a private yacht and we're sailing to San Diego."

"How adventurous! Is it just the two of you?"

"Oh no." Doug replied, "We have a seven-man crew with four passengers."

"That sounds like a large ship!" Ann exclaimed.

Doug answered proudly, "Yes, it's 120 feet."

"Does a movie star own it?" asked Ann.

"No, the owner is a CEO of a large corporation. When we come into port, he treats us to a couple of nights on shore while he stays with the boat."

Ann and I immediately realized that Dan had made the reservations for this couple in his name. Doug continued, "But before you feel sorry for the guy, you should see his stateroom!"

Just then, the elevator door opened. We all stepped out and said our good-byes. Then Ann and I headed in the opposite direction; I didn't want to be at the front desk when they walked by just in case the clerk pointed me out.

Meeting the captain and his wife had been a little inconvenient, since we sure didn't want them to blow the whistle on us. Even so, we had learned something more about our quarry and that was helpful. We left the hotel, camera loaded, and headed for the marina. José met us there. We relayed what we had learned in the elevator and José put two men on duty to watch the yacht twenty-four hours a day.

A full day passed and the only movement had been a few deckhands going on and off board. Rather than just wait around in Panama City, Ann and I decided to get ahead of "The Rover" by a few days. So we set out for her next stop, Acapulco.

Days went by, the estimated arrival time for "The Rover" came and went, and we started to get nervous. "Well, dear, looks as though we'll have to head north to Cabo San Lucas," I said.

"Oh, do we have to?" moaned Ann, with a twinkle in her eye.

"Yeah, I know it's tough, but someone has to do it."

Dan was losing time. He wasn't following his itinerary, and we began to wonder where he was going to drop off his "first mate." We felt it had to be Acapulco or Cabo, because the next stop would be San Diego. Surely he wouldn't have the balls to take her into the homeport! Then again, maybe that was his scheme. He'd show up and put his lover on a plane back to Miami before his wife even knew he was in town.

I was impressed. Real gutsy, if this was his plan.

Off we went to Cabo. We arrived at the Marina de la Gloria, which overlooks the harbor, unpacked our bags, and dressed in shorts and sandals. We called the harbormaster and asked if they had heard from "The Rover." No word yet. Another two days passed, and still no sign. Damn! Could I have miscalculated the speed and distance? We couldn't ask the harbormaster too many times, or he'd get suspicious and tell the captain that someone had been asking about them.

"What's our plan now?" asked Ann.

I wished I had Ann's ability to take things in stride. She doesn't get rattled and stays focused. I, on the other hand, beat things to death trying to find out why something is or isn't happening. I come up with scenarios and brainstorm them with whoever will listen … usually Ann. She will sit back, and then feed me her impressions. If they match up with mine (which they usually do), we act on them.

We mulled over the idea that maybe the lovebirds weren't stopping at Acapulco and Cabo. Maybe they were going to go straight through to San Diego. But it didn't make sense that they would hurry past all the romantic ports of call only to rush to San Diego, and the arms of Paula.

After a couple of days and no sign of "The Rover," Ann suggested we call Acapulco, the harbormaster in Cabo, and the marina at Coronado Island in San Diego Bay to see if any of them had heard from Dan and his party. Saturday morning I sat down at the phone and began calling. The last call was to the marina at Coronado Island. They said they expected the yacht to arrive that evening. Oh shit! I turned towards Ann, who was lying on the bed facing me. She could tell by my expression I was drained of life force.

We discussed what to do and decided I should call Tracy, who lives in Los Angeles and works part-time for me and part-time as a driver for the Hollywood elite. I got Tracy on his cellular phone and asked if he could drive to San Diego and videotape a group of people leaving a luxury yacht. He said he could be there in four hours. I gave him my cellular number, along with a description of Dan, and told him that Dan would be wearing a young woman on his arm, so there would probably be an abundance of kissing and groping. And that's what we were after.

After I hung up the phone, I turned to Ann. "Let's go out on the town tonight and celebrate our misfortune. I know Tracy will give it his best shot. I just wish we could have nailed this guy ourselves."

We made flight reservations to leave the next morning for San Diego. Then I called Paula to bring her up to date. She is a true lady and didn't appear to be as frustrated as one would expect. In fact, she said we'd done an excellent job at being in all the places that "The Rover" was supposed to be. It wasn't our fault that Dan didn't show his face.

This was only slightly comforting to Ann and me because we don't generally spend this amount of time and energy and not get the goods. I ended the conversation with Paula by telling her it wasn't over yet. I felt certain Tracy would come through for us.

That last evening in Cabo started off as though we were going to the funeral of a close friend. We tried our best to enjoy ourselves and dressed for a night of colorful music and dance. After dinner, we were heading towards the dance floor when my cellular phone rang. It was Tracy. I went outside where I could hear him better.

"You won't believe what I have to report."

"Go ahead."

"I talked to Carol, the captain's wife. She was waiting on the dock for her husband to finish shutting down the yacht and come ashore with the dingy. I could tell she had a little too much to drink because she was very talkative. I decided this would be an excellent chance to ask her if she knew where Dan was. She said that Dan had flown to Cabo from Panama City and was staying there through the weekend. She went on to tell me he was with Sharon, *his niece!*"

Tracy laughed as he continued, "Carol said Dan and his 'niece' were soaking up the sun and margaritas at the Marina de la Gloria."

"Tracy, you hit a home run! Thanks. I'll call you when I get home."

I went back in and found Ann sitting at our table watching the dancers. "You won't believe this! Dan is HERE with his girlfriend. He'll be leaving Monday for San Diego."

"What? He's here in Cabo?"

"That's what Tracy says. Let's find him!"

Ann went upstairs to get a bird's eye view of the club. As soon as she reached the top, she immediately turned around and walked back down, smiling. What had she seen? She took my hand, led me outside, and told me to look directly across from where we had been sitting. There was Dan, looking deep into the eyes of a young brunette as they sipped Piña Coladas.

I told Ann to stay and watch over our lovebirds while I went to get the cameras. When I came back, Ann was in the hotel lobby and Dan and Sharon were at the front desk asking for messages. I handed the cameras to Ann and she sat down in a high-back wicker chair. As I walked over to the reservations desk, I was just in time to see the clerk pull a piece a paper from a box-marked #234. Ann and I were in #272. When the clerk turned to me, I asked if there were any messages for Room 272.

Ann came up behind me and we followed Dan and Sharon up the stairs to their room. As we neared #234, I whispered a plan in Ann's ear. She was to go and stand at the next room opening so she could capture the lovebirds going into their room. I would walk around them to get their attention and excuse myself. That way Ann could get a front shot of them when they turned in my direction.

It all came together like clockwork. Dan and Sharon slowed down to put the key in the door, and I came up behind them and said, "Excuse me" as I walked past them. They both turned towards me. I knew Ann had gotten a great shot of them as they turned my direction and then entered their room. Keeping the hidden video camera running, she walked by the room with them inside. We continued down the hall to the end and then walked back, passing their room on the way to ours.

Ann and I had a very peaceful evening celebrating our success. We just felt bad that Tracy couldn't join us.

Since we still had Sunday and maybe a half day on Monday to get film on Dan and Sharon before we returned to San Diego, Ann decided to get friendly with Sharon. That way she could find out more about her, perhaps get her last name and address.

We awoke bright and early Sunday and enjoyed a continental breakfast in the lounge. At 11:10 Dan and Sharon finally showed up and ordered some coffee. We took a few snapshots of them holding hands and kissing. We were sitting close enough to hear them making plans for the day. Sharon wanted to go shopping. It was apparent she wanted to spend some of that community property!

Ann volunteered to follow Dan and Sharon all day. Not wanting to follow two people shopping all day, I agreed and went back to our room to get some serious siesta time.

Just after 4:00 Ann returned to our room loaded down with shopping bags full of souvenirs for our kids and our home. She took the videotape out of the camera and connected it to the television in our room. We watched what we had taped the night before—Dan fondling Sharon while they sat, walked, and talked. He had his hands everywhere! Then we watched them enter their hotel room.

All of a sudden, the film showed Dan saying to Ann, "Hi, I'm Dan and this is my bride, Sharon. We're here in Cabo on our honeymoon." My chin dropped to the floor. "How did you do that?" I exclaimed.

"I just got friendly with Sharon and she told me about her romance with Dan. She said they got married in Florida and were spending their honeymoon in Cabo. In fact," she turned to me with a smug smile on her face, "we're having dinner with them tonight!"

This was too good to be true. He admitted to marrying Sharon on tape and gave Paula ironclad evidence against him. But it didn't make the task ahead of her any easier. Ann had found out that Sharon would return to Florida from Cabo to search for a new house, while Dan would be returning to San Diego at the same time as us.

Ann filled me in on our game plan for the upcoming evening. We met the newlyweds in the lobby, and then shared a cab to the Rosarita, a fine eating establishment up the coast from Cabo. We had the restaurant photographer take a group picture at our table. Dan was gracious and pleasant to be around—until he started drinking. I've met men like Dan before; very arrogant, self-indulgent, and successful because they never put limits on anything they do. Whether its sports, gambling, women, or business, they are constantly taking chances.

The following day we said goodbye to the "new bride," Sharon, as she left for Florida. We couldn't help noticing how sweet and trusting she was with this man she called her husband. It was a tragedy for her, as well as for Paula.

There was nothing more to be accomplished, so we flew out an hour later for San Diego. We knew Paula would be pleased and devastated by our work. Both women were victims. I felt especially sorry for Sharon, who had poured out her heart and soul for this man. At least Paula had the years of cheating and misery to fall back on.

When confronted, Dan admitted he was a bigamist. In return for their promise not to pursue bigamy charges against him, Paula and Sharon received generous settlements. Dan tried to get away with something he truly believed would work: a wife on each coast. Last we heard, he had retired and set sail for ports unknown. Alone.

3

The Other Woman

Irene had been married for four years to Ron, a handsome man in his early thirties. Irene had an inheritance that would make the rich envious. Ron, on the other hand, came from a working class family and never extended his formal education beyond high school. He was employed as a car salesman for a large dealership in Oakland. Irene was a full-time teacher with the local school system.

Ron and Irene had a grand marriage ceremony, followed by a huge reception for 500 guests. The bride was gorgeous with her luxurious blonde hair and big blue eyes, her face framed by the lacy collar of her white gown. The groom, with his dark hair, blue eyes, and rich tan, could easily have passed for a movie star.

But after only four years the honeymoon was over. Ron started coming home from work later and later in the evening, and there were frequent hang-ups on the home phone. In a casual conversation with her girlfriend, Irene said she was beginning to have suspicions that Ron was seeing someone else (although like many women, she found this hard to believe). The girlfriend told Irene the signs were all there and urged her to contact a private investigator to be certain.

This is where I came in. Irene said she and her mother were about to leave on a cruise; and she wanted me to follow Ron while they were gone. After gathering some information, I agreed to take the assignment.

Irene had said it might be difficult to follow Ron because, as a car dealer, he could drive any car on the lot. I didn't fully realize the impact of her words until the first night of my surveillance. As I waited by the underground garage, I saw a dozen vehicles drive away, all going in different directions. I picked a car I thought might be Ron's, but quickly found out I was mistaken. Scratch that surveillance.

I decided to drive to Ron and Irene's home in the Lafayette foothills and wait for Ron to arrive. By midnight, he hadn't shown up. I noted this for Irene. The following morning, I got up early and drove back to the house. Still no sign of Ron or his car.

Then I had an idea. I would make an appointment with him to look at a new car. No, forget that. I needed someone he would never see again. Then I remembered Marsha, a woman I met at the athletic club I belong to. She had said many times how fascinating she thought my work was, and frequently offered to help on a case. Here was her chance! I would have her meet with Ron and ask him to show her a new car. And I'd have her go in just before the lot closed. Since Ron wouldn't be able to leave right at closing, I'd have a good shot of following him. Perfect!

I contacted Marsha and she willingly agreed to help out. I set up surveillance with my colleague, Tracy, between Broadway and Harrison Streets where we both had good views of the car lot. Marsha went in just a few minutes before the lot closed for the evening and asked the manager for Ron.

Ron came strolling up to Marsha. "Hi, may I help you?"

"Yes. I was told by Greg to see you if I needed a new car."

Ron replied that he was the used car manager, meaning that he only sold used cars. Slightly flustered, Marsha quickly rebounded, "Oh, I'm sorry. I didn't make myself clear. When I said 'new car;' I meant a 'new-to-me' car. You know — a used car."

"Well, in that case, I'm the one to talk to. What are you looking for?"

"A reliable, well maintained car."

"We have lots to choose from and I'd be happy to show you what we have, but we're closing for the night. Can you come back tomorrow?"

Marsha agreed and asked for Ron's business card. As he took down her name and phone number, Marsha asked him if there was a nice place nearby to meet a friend for drinks. Ron recommended two spots, a place on Jack London Square or Oscars by the lake. Marsha left and stopped by my car to return the wire she had been wearing. Marsha's job was over. Mine was just beginning.

A station wagon left the garage shortly after that. I felt fairly confident it was Ron, so Tracy and I each followed the car as it headed up to MacArthur Boulevard, south to Lakeshore, and then around Lake Merritt to Oscar's. Bingo!

Ron parked across the street from the restaurant and crossed the intersection right in front of Tracy's car. I thought grimly to myself that Tracy could save Irene a lot of heartache by just running over Ron. Tracy found a place to park, and I went around the block so I could park on the same side of the street as the restaurant. We entered the establishment and saw there was a hofbrau-style dining area on the right. Straight ahead, there was a round fireplace surrounded by small tables. We also saw tables set up against the far walls.

We noticed Ron sitting with five young men in business suits. They all looked like used car salesmen—nicely dressed and eager. The men left one-by-one until there was only Ron and another young man about his age still at the table. They stayed for one more round and left around 11:20 p.m.

Tracy walked out first and heard Ron say to the unidentified male, "I'll follow you, Steve." Both men hopped in their cars and sped away. Tracy and I didn't follow because it was too late for them to get lucky, and it was apparent from their parting words they were going to do something together. We called it a night.

The next evening, we went through the same scenario. We followed the guys to Oscar's. They had a few drinks. Late in the evening they took off with Ron following Steve.

"That's it," I told Tracy. "Tomorrow we'll follow them wherever they're going!"

The next day was a Saturday and, to our dismay, we discovered it was Ron's day off. So we took off for his Lafayette home. He wasn't there. Damn!

The weekend went by and we still hadn't learned whom Ron was seeing. On Monday evening we again set up surveillance at Oscar's. This time my wife, Ann, joined us. She and I waited outside. Tracy was inside the restaurant and was to let us know the moment it seemed that Ron was leaving.

At 10:40 p.m., Tracy called and said the two were paying
their bill and would be out soon. Ann hopped into her car and
I started mine. There they were. Steve honked his horn at
Ron as he took off. Ron honked back with a wave. The three
of us followed Ron as he drove straight home, parked his car
in the garage, and went into the house. It was 11:15 p.m., and
we sat there with egg on our faces. I asked Tracy if he saw
anything unusual while staking them out, and got a negative
response. "They did what they always do. They drank and
talked and were the last to leave, as always. No hitting on
women. Nothing!"

With our client coming back Friday, we had four days left
to find something out. I told Tracy we would see him tomorrow and if he got to Oakland first, he could feel free to follow
Ron if he spotted him leaving.

At 9:00 Tuesday evening, the three of us surrounded the
auto dealership as the cars started coming out from the
underground garage. Tracy took after a Volvo coupe and Ann
and I stayed put, hoping to see Ron leave. Finally, the place
looked deserted. I picked up my cell phone and called to see
if Ron was still there and was told that he had left about ten
minutes ago. I put in a call to Tracy. He told me he was just
getting out of his car to go into Scott's, a fashionable seafood
restaurant and bar at Jack London Square. After a few minutes, he called me to say Ron was there with his usual crowd.

Ann and I headed over to Scott's. As we walked in, we saw
the group in a far corner. Then we spotted Tracy. He was at a
table for four that was at a slightly higher elevation and gave
us an ideal view of Ron and his group. I smiled and patted
Tracy on the shoulder. "Good work, Tracy! Ann and I didn't
see Ron leave. We're lucky you did."

The evening's events progressed exactly as they had at Oscar's. The time wore on and the guys began to leave. Again, it was just Ron and Steve at the table. "Now," I said to Tracy and Ann, "let's hope they go off together so we can follow them." Ann's voice was oddly sure as she stated, "Oh, there won't be a problem there."

Tracy and I looked at the men enjoying their drinks and talking. I turned to Ann, "What do you mean?" I asked. "What do you see?"

I've learned that Ann, being a woman, sees things we guys tend to overlook. "Well, for one thing, I see Ron's little finger touching Steve's little finger. Secondly, Steve is looking at Ron the way a woman looks at her lover … all dreamy eyed."

I looked at the two men again.

"Oh shit! It's true!" I exclaimed. Leave it to a woman to pick up on something that subtle.

This time when Ron and Steve left, we followed them to Steve's place in Berkeley. It was a small corner apartment overlooking Shattuck Ave. We were able to videotape the men going inside—hand-in-hand! We saw the lights go on, and someone came to the curtain and looked out onto the empty streets below. A light in the back came on. The front light went out. Finally, about thirty minutes later, the back room light went out.

This case was just about closed, but how do you tell your client the 'other woman' in her husband's life is really a man?

Irene called on Friday evening after returning from her cruise. She sounded real positive over the phone. "Did you find out anything on Ron? Do we talk now or in person?" she asked.

When I told her that we needed to sit and talk face to face, she hesitated for just an instant. "OK. Sure. But why do you sound so mysterious, Greg?"

"I think these things go better when you can get the play-by-play report in person. Also, Tracy and Ann will be present so if you have any questions, it might be easier to answer them."

We decided to meet at her house at 3 o'clock the following afternoon; it was Ron's Saturday to work. Irene and her mother were waiting for us. Irene offered us a cold soft drink and pretzels. Finally, she asked the big question, "Well, how did it go?"

I started by relaying how Tracy and I had set up surveillance the first few days at the dealership, but had lost sight of Ron. I told her about Marsha's help and about Ron recommending the two restaurants.

"Yes, Ron used to take me there," Irene offered.

"That's where we caught up with him night after night. He'd meet several guys there, but it was always Ron and Steve that stayed the longest. They would always leave together."

"Did they pick up girls? Is that what you're trying to say?"

"No, I'm not. What I'm trying to say is that Steve may be more than just a friend to Ron."

Irene looked perplexed. "What do you mean?"

Ann spoke up, "What we're trying to say is that we have pretty good evidence that Ron and Steve are lovers."

"No! That can't be. Not Ron!"

Ann continued, "Irene, I was on the last two nights of surveillance and I saw Ron and Steve's fingertips touching while they were having drinks at Scott's. Steve gave every indication that he was infatuated with Ron. Afterwards, we followed them to Steve's apartment. They went upstairs together and within thirty minutes, all the lights went out, including the bedroom light. They were seen together every evening after work, and Ron came home only one night in the last week. You're just going to have to confront him on this and see what he has to say. We have a video of Ron and Steve walking hand-in-hand to Steve's apartment."

Irene started crying. "Oh God, this can't be happening!" Irene's mother embraced her daughter and they both began to weep. Finally, Irene's mother confided that she had suspected there was something 'different' about Ron. "Looking back, it all makes sense," she said.

Irene looked totally defeated. "Mom, how do I fight a thing like this? How do I compete against another man?"

At the time this case occurred, HIV was thought to be predominantly a homosexual disease. Irene immediately had herself tested. Fortunately, the results were negative for the virus.

Ron and Irene divorced. Ron came out of the closet and was a happier person living his life with Steve. Although Ron and Irene realized they couldn't stay married, they remained friends. They worked together to understand the new feelings they were experiencing. Above all, they accepted the fact that no one was at fault for the failure of their marriage.

4

When to Hire A Professional

I received a call from one of those women who are used to controlling a situation. Men call them "bitches" and women call them "assertive." She was in her early thirties, armed with a master's degree in business administration, and married to an entrepreneurial powerhouse named Dave. They met while attending classes at Stanford and religiously followed the same routine every morning: rise at 6:00 a.m., jog ten miles, grab some toast and juice, followed by an aerobic exercise program, shower, and dress to make money! This couple owned over 100 boutiques in every state in the Union, and a few in Canada and England. They led such a regimented life that there was no room for children, vacations, or idle conversation. I know because I tried to have a friendly little chat with Lisa and was abruptly cut off.

Lisa had medium blonde hair parked on top of her head in a tidy chignon. She wore a tailored suit and no-frills blouse, accented by a red tie that could not be described as a bow or ribbon. This was definitely one of those "power suits." High heels and a small briefcase completed the ensemble. She gave the impression of a successful woman in complete control, and she didn't want anything from me except advice.

She gave me the basic facts about her seven-year marriage to Dave. During the entire seven years he had been not only her husband, but a true friend and partner. However, during the past few months she had become aware of a change in his personality that was in contrast to their usual lifestyle. He exercised constantly when he wasn't working, and his working hours had slowed to a trickle in these last months.

"He used to put in at least 16 hours a day and he has dropped that down to 10 or 12 hours, which is not the work ethic we both agreed to when we started our marriage and company," Lisa added. "I'm doing most of the work now, and he's leaving a mess for me to clean up. I think he's seeing one of our managers in San Diego. We have a store in La Jolla and he's been spending far too much time down there. I want to hire you to tell me what I need to know so that I can catch him myself. I don't want to be sitting at home. I want to face him head on!

"Dave informed me last night that he's planning to leave for San Diego on a 7:00 a.m. flight next Thursday, and that he'll be back home on Sunday. I know there's no reason for him to go back there after being there last week, and then it was for two days longer than necessary. I'm all too familiar with our store manager in La Jolla. She looks just like Melanie Griffith, and Dave always tells me how beautiful Melanie Griffith is. Dave hired Melanie's look alike, including the sweet little girl voice."

"Let's take this one step at a time," I suggested. "First, you must have someone you trust to help you. Do you have a friend who would go with you?"

"Yes!"

"Secondly," I went on and paused. "Are you writing this down?"

"I have a great memory," came the tart reply. Why don't you dispense with telling me about the routines I need to follow and instead provide me with a written, detailed outline. Here is a cash retainer. You can jot down a receipt of sorts now and submit a formal receipt later. We have six days before he leaves. I'll expect to hear from you no later than Tuesday. I want a complete breakdown on surveillance and anything you can try to predict that will help us."

I usually control these meetings and I'm not used to being told to sit down and listen. Well, it's her dime. I wondered if she scheduled their sex life. Everyone shows their anger and pain in their own way. Some people just come on stronger when they're under attack.

At this point Lisa handed me her husband's itinerary, a description and home address of the La Jolla manager, a description of her car, and the address of their boutique in La Jolla. I returned to the office and began thinking of all the details needed to set up surveillance in San Diego. First, Lisa would need communication between vehicles, and that's something we'd need to order beforehand. I placed a call to a fellow PI and friend in San Diego and asked whom he rented communications equipment from down there. Jim recommended a few businesses that had mobile and portable handheld units. I gave them a call and found one with a repeater site, which would cover San Diego to Carlsbad.

I called the company and ordered the radios to be picked up Thursday afternoon. I secured the deal with my credit card, and he faxed back the confirmation and rental price. Then I punched up San Diego County on my computer and began printing copies of street maps of the area surrounding the boutique and the area where Jill lived in Mission Bay. I even highlighted a few common routes that one might use to go back and forth from these two addresses.

I now had files with the headings COMMUNICATIONS and TERRITORY Only a dossier on DISGUISES remained, and this was easy to complete. It was a detailed shopping list, which I prefaced with the following:

To: Lisa and her partner:

Both of you may be required to enter a nightspot. Dress as though you're trying to impress a man. Jill certainly is. Lisa, you must totally change your appearance in every way. Your friend, if unknown to David, can go "as is." However, neither of you can be recognized by David, even close up.

I also attached a list of what they would need to pull this off, each of the items needing to be brand new:

- *Wig that is both different color and style*
- *Dress or short skirts for evening wear*
- *High-heeled shoes for evening out*
- *Tennis shoes for driving and outside surveillance*
- *Two pair of eyeglasses, one clear and one dark*
- *8mm handheld video camera*
- *Large purse to carry walkie-talkie and camera*
- *Mustache*

- *Mole or beauty spot*
- *Binoculars*

Another file was entitled TAILING. I covered the fine points of placing someone under surveillance and how to follow him or her so they won't get suspicious. I outlined the importance of each operative needing to be on opposite sides of a street so they can successfully follow the suspect no matter which way he may travel. And if you have a choice, follow the female, not the male. Take turns being the car in front, and never confront your prey eye-to-eye. Never appear that you're interested in them. Bring a book along to appear as though you're reading when the traveling gets slow. If forced to share an elevator, beat them to the buttons. Tip valets and hosts a twenty to be seated near your quarry's table or to have your car parked near the front for fast getaways.

The VIDEOTAPING file covered how to videotape, lighting, zoom, sound, covering that blinking red light, and taping without making fast, jerky moves. And of paramount importance: always carry spare, fully charged batteries.

After spending many hours pouring out the wisdom gained over 18 years, I was ready to give her outline the finishing touches. "WHAT TO DO IF MURPHY'S LAW GOES INTO EFFECT?" A "How-To" of finding someone after you've lost him or her in traffic and the grid-by-grid search. Where it's most likely you'll be able to catch the "grope" on video: parking lots, dance floors, front door of his hotel, front door of her house or apartment, and in the car at a long red light.

Now was the time to talk to her again. I didn't want to wait until Tuesday because she would be in too much of a rush to finish everything. If she were going to be successful, I would have to take some of the pressure off her. I purchased two video cameras with two long-playing batteries and binoculars, and then Ann and I contacted Lisa to tell her that she needed to begin preparations now before she flew to San Diego. I told her I had finished my outline and had purchased the cameras and binoculars. She was relieved and appreciative, and her demeanor had improved substantially. She stated that it was so hectic at work that she hoped her girlfriend would handle most of the preparations.

We scheduled another meeting at the Brass Door. She seemed to be more at ease. I gave her my outline and warned her of some of the pitfalls that she may come across. I told her she needed to go by the "communications shop" before noon and have them install antennas in both cars and show her how to operate the equipment. Lisa took off on Thursday for San Diego, as expected. I left my number to call me if she got in a bind.

The weekend went by and I hadn't heard from Lisa. A few more weeks went by, so I called her and made arrangements to get together at the Brass Door. Lisa looked just as she had before, but I noticed a change immediately in her personality. She was more feminine and sensitive. I asked her how it went with the surveillance. She looked sheepish and said, "It didn't. I screwed the whole thing up."

Lisa prefaced her tale by assuring me that my instructions had worked incredibly well. They arrived at the boutique just before closing and spotted Jill. She was closing the store; and, of course, David was in the shop ... helping. They took their respective cars and drove to the Chart House restaurant in La Jolla, parking in a nearby garage.

"Carol and I entered the restaurant after a few minutes, and I offered the maitre d' a twenty, as you suggested, but

Dave and Jill had already been seated between two occupied tables. I told the maitre d' to seat us behind them when a table became available, which it did twenty minutes later.

"I knew my disguise worked well because Dave looked right at me and gave me the once over. What a relief! We sat together even though you told me to develop a triangle in the restaurant. I was so nervous!

"Carol ordered so Dave wouldn't hear my voice. Then we sat back and listened to his bullshit about how domineering and frigid I am. He even told her that he had to make an appointment with me a month ahead of time for sex."

Have you ever been drinking wine and had it back up your nose? Boy, did I call that one!

Then the story became funnier. Lisa and Carol timed their departure just prior to the completion of the lovebirds' meal. They followed them to Jill's new Mission Bay town-house. So new, in fact, that she hadn't put draperies or curtains up yet. Carol and Lisa waited outside and watched from a row of trees in the courtyard. They could see Dave and Jill in the kitchen pouring wine and kissing, before walking upstairs.

"We saw the bedroom light go on," she said, "and just knew they had to be getting undressed." Lisa pulled out her 8mm camera and placed the strap over her right wrist. She didn't think of changing into her tennis shoes. The adrenaline was pumping, and her heart was pounding. She was a woman on a mission. Lisa began climbing the nearest tree, clearing the lower branches and was oh so close to seeing into the window.

"Just as I spotted asshole's head I heard the branch I was standing on snap. I couldn't help it—I let out a scream. The next thing I felt was a sharp pain going right up my right cheek and then up my back. Windows and doors were opening; lights were shining, searching for the source of the continuing screams. I had totally lost my composure. I was screaming to the top of my lungs. My wig was hanging off the side of my head and the camera had dropped out of my hand. Carol was climbing up the tree to help me, but her high-heeled shoe got stuck half way up. Now this fucking tree was swaying side to side and my skirt was up around my boobs. My pantyhose were ripped and a branch managed to catch my panties and make a thong out of them. My makeup was running down my face; and while I'm screaming, I see the asshole I'm married to putting on his pants and getting the hell out of there!

"Within ten minutes policemen are looking up Carol's and my legs. We're both traumatized by the fucking experience; and to make it worse, when the fire department arrived they used a cherry picker to pull us off the tree. The police took our names and IDs, and then knocked on the bitch's door to ask her if she wanted to press charges against us for invasion of privacy.

"I stood there in front of her, absolutely humiliated; and what's more, I can't even fire the bitch. So in answer to your question ... well, that's how it went!"

I guess I should have told her about tree climbing in heels and the public's distaste for peeping Toms.

Lisa continued. "I got home early the following morning and the son of a bitch was already gone. When I did catch up to him at lunch he denied going out with her. His version of his time with Lisa was that he had helped her at the store, they had a quick bite after work, and he came straight home. The nerve of that lying shit."

"Hold on," I said. "First of all, that's the funniest story I've ever heard. And secondly, you know that was him in bed, right? What other proof do you need?"

"I don't have a videotape of it, and my girlfriend didn't see shit. I wonder if I really saw him, or did I see someone who looks like him? I'll never know for sure."

"Next time, you'll hire a professional?"

"No shit. You said it!"

There is a positive ending to this tale of humiliation. Lisa has Dave on a very short leash! He knows that she knows, and he knows he better knock it off.

Lisa, I'll be waiting for your next call.

5

How They
Hide the Money

Joyce contacted me in July and said she had a friend that might need my help. (Now where have I heard that one before?)

"What kind of help?" I asked.

"She thinks her husband is having an affair and she needs to prove it. She also needs to get into his office and look over his records to see what he might be hiding."

"Okay," I replied, "I'll meet with her. Tell her to bring a photograph of her husband, his office address, office phone number, and so on, as well as any information she has about the woman he may be having an affair with."

"How much is all of this going to cost?"

"I can't answer that question until I have more information. After we talk I'll be able to provide some figures."

We arranged for me to meet with Trudy, Joyce's friend, at 11 o'clock the next morning at the Lafayette Park Hotel for coffee. I asked Joyce if she would be joining us. I expected the answer to be a resounding "No," but was surprised at her answer.

"Oh yes, I'll be there. I doubt Trudy will meet with you if I don't come along."

I sure had that one figured wrong. I can't tell you how many times a person calls about the problems of a "mystery friend" and eventually confesses to being the person who needs the help.

I watched Trudy and Joyce drive up to the Lafayette Park Hotel in a Ford Explorer. Both women appeared to be in their early thirties. As they approached me, I noticed their attractive tans and healthy appearances. They looked like they had just come off the tennis court or golf course.

Since Joyce had been the mouthpiece for Trudy, I expected Trudy to be nervous about our meeting. I was wrong again. She wasn't nervous at all.

Trudy told me about her 14-year marriage to Gene, and how they had built a very successful insurance firm from scratch. She began to suspect he was having an affair with the wife of a local car dealer—a blonde, older woman. She reached into her purse and pulled out a photograph taken at a party. She identified a handsome, very slender man in the picture as her husband. She also pointed to an attractive blonde woman standing next to an older, balding man.

"Is that her?" I asked.

"It sure is!"

Trudy handed me a note pad on which she had written the addresses and telephone numbers of where the woman lived and worked. She also provided me with Gene's office address and telephone number, and a description of his car. We agreed on a retainer amount, which she immediately paid, in cash.

"I need to take a look at your husband's office before I can commit to being able to getting you in. Are you absolutely sure there's no key around?"

"Believe me; I've searched the entire house more than once. He's also told me—more than once—that he doesn't want me coming by the office. He's going to be at a business meeting on Friday night and won't be home until late. Do you think we can go in then?"

"I'll need to check out the office, so let me call you," I instructed. "In the meantime, you get the telephone number where he's going to be and then we can call him right before we leave. You're absolutely sure it's a business meeting he's going to and he won't be home until late?"

Trudy reassured me she was positive about the extended meeting. "O.K., I'll call Joyce after I've had an opportunity to check out the office."

That afternoon, I drove by Gene's office in San Ramon. His car was parked in the back near his private entrance. I looked the place over and discovered there were no security alarms or anything! This would be a piece of cake. I called Joyce back and told her Friday night was fine with me. Then I called Burt, one of my assistants, and he agreed to be my "eye man" while I picked the lock.

Friday night arrived and Joyce called at 9:10. She told me they were ready if I was. We met at the Brass Door in San Ramon. Both ladies were dressed in summery loose smocks. Joyce was decked out in a blue flowered print and Trudy was wearing vivid shades of red. I wondered if they had been at a Hawaiian theme party or just decided to dress alike on purpose. I couldn't help but notice the anxiety in their faces as I asked, "Are you ladies ready?" They nodded and Trudy said, "Let's get on with it."

Burt followed us in his own car to Gene's office. I parked my car in the back and had Burt locate himself where he had the best view of the entire office complex. I left Trudy and Joyce to walk over to Burt's car.

"Now, if you see anything at all, tell me … okay?"

"Don't worry," he assured me.

I went over the game plan with Burt and then added, "We'll sit in the car until you give us the all-clear." He nodded his agreement.

I returned to my car and sat quietly with Trudy and Joyce. It was only a few minutes later when I heard Burt's voice through my earpiece. "There's not anyone around for a hundred miles. Go for it!"

My first job was to open the door. I started by placing my pick in the lock. Then I placed a pressure tool underneath the lock to give me leverage. I turned the tumblers until I had them aligned. It only took a few strokes and the lock was opened. I motioned to Trudy and Joyce to follow me in, and I informed Burt we were ready to enter the office.

Our first task was to search the file cabinets. They were all locked so I had pick them open—all eight of them. I completed the job in just under five minutes! Then I sat down at Gene's cherry wood desk. Each of the three drawers was individually locked … with good reason, I suspected. Click, click, click and I had them open. In the top right drawer was a safety box containing keys from a bank. In the next drawer was an envelope containing nude pictures of Trudy and the blonde. There were at least a dozen pictures of both women.

"Joyce, can you come here, please?" I asked.

Joyce came over immediately and Trudy rushed after her. I handed Joyce the bank keys and asked her to hand them to

Trudy. Trudy asked what they were, and I said I thought they looked like safety deposit box keys.

"Great! But to where?" she asked.

"If you check the file cabinets, we may find out."

Trudy rushed back to the file cabinets and Joyce went with her. I tucked the photographs in my coat pocket. As I continued my inspection of the desk drawers, I came across the identity of the banks where Gene held safety deposit boxes. I told Joyce to make a copy of everything they needed.

"Oh, and Joyce, copy these too." I handed her the photographs from my coat pocket. She let out a small gasp and whispered, "Oh, my!"

After Joyce finished copying the photographs, she handed them to Trudy, who immediately sucked all the air out of the room. She turned in my direction, but being a gentleman to a fault, I pretended not to notice.

We completed our search and made copies of anything that looked suspicious, including two sets of books, one for the IRS and one for business loans. Trudy handed the photograph originals back to me. "You better put these back where you found them." I couldn't help but notice her blushing face.

I contacted Burt and told him we were about ready to leave and asked, "Is it safe?"

"All clear," Burt replied.

Trudy and Joyce ran out to the car. I lingered behind to be sure everything was left the way we had found it. I noticed the copy machine was not reset to "0," so I did that. All of the file cabinets were locked and so was Gene's desk. Lights out, and then I re-locked the door to Gene's office.

We returned to the Brass Door and had a drink to celebrate our success. Trudy wanted us to follow Gene on Monday and get some videotape of him with Bonnie, the other woman. On Monday morning, I followed Bonnie from her home in Walnut Creek to the Best Western on Clayton Road. Burt staked out Gene's office and contacted me by two-way radio to let me know that Gene had just left and was most likely on his way.

Sure enough, the loving couple met at the Best Western where Gene made arrangements for a room. I was able to videotape Gene leaving the rental office with the room key in his hand, walking around back to meet Bonnie, and both of them entering the room.

Four hours later they surfaced. Gene walked Bonnie to her car, stopping along the way for some quick kisses and butt pats. Then he returned the key to the rental office with Burt and me watching his every move. As he headed for his car, we noticed he threw what appeared to be the receipt in a nearby trashcan. After he drove off, Burt strolled by and retrieved the receipt. We wrote our report for Trudy and included the videotape and the receipt.

Five months later I heard from Trudy. She brought me up to date on what had happened.

After receiving our report and video, she had waited until after dinner before confronting Gene. Without telling him about the investigation, she simply asked if he had any intentions of divorcing her. Gene seemed perplexed.

"Are you kidding? What are you talking about?"

"Aren't you having an affair with Bonnie?"

"Are you nuts?"

"Gene, I'm not asking you if you're having an affair. I'm telling you you're having an affair."

"Damn it Trudy, for God's sake, get a life!" Gene exclaimed. "I can't imagine where you come up with this garbage!"

With that, Trudy pointed the remote to the television. In living color and on the big screen, there was Gene kissing Bonnie in the parking lot ... Gene escorting Bonnie to their room ... and then, four hours later (as displayed on the video), Gene walking Bonnie to her car.

Gene lowered his head, walked over to the television, and turned it off. He had tears in his eyes as he turned towards Trudy. "Oh God, I'm so embarrassed! And relieved it's over. The pressure has been awful, worrying that you would find out. Trudy, I love you more than anything. I can't tell you why I did it. I don't know why. Please believe me when I say it's over now."

"Were you planning on leaving me and marrying her?"

"No! No! Where would you get an idea like that?"

"Maybe from the fact you've been hiding money from me in your own special accounts and in bank deposit boxes! What do you have to say about that?"

Gene replied sheepishly, "I was afraid if you ever caught me you would take everything and leave me penniless."

"So, instead, you thought you would leave *me* penniless, right?" Trudy shouted.

"No, not at all! If you'll just give me another chance, I'll turn over every dime I have. That's how much I love you. Please. I want another chance," Gene begged.

"Okay," said Trudy, with an air of confidence. "I'll have my attorney draw up the paperwork." Trudy said she had suspected that Gene would react this way, so she had already consulted with an attorney.

"Whatever you want. Oh, Trudy, I love you so much. I'll do anything."

And he did. All of their assets were placed in Trudy's name—all signed, recorded, and legal.

The best part of this story? Trudy and Gene are still married and happy. In fact, Trudy says it's like being newlyweds again.

The happy ending is largely due to Trudy's having done a lot of things right. She kept quiet about the suspected affair until she had all her ducks in a row. When the pendulum swung in her favor—in other words, she had Gene by the balls—she used her newfound assertiveness to make her demands.

- She didn't give Gene a lot of time to think about the situation.

- She consulted with an attorney beforehand to be sure she knew her rights.

- Before confronting Gene, she knew where and what their assets were.

6

'Tis the Season

I have often been asked if my job as a private investigator is seasonal. It sure seems like it! My phone starts ringing off the hook beginning in October and continues right through to the New Year.

One case that immediately comes to mind involves a philandering husband, Fred, telling Dana, his unsuspecting wife, that due to poor sales, the annual employees' Christmas party would be just that this year—for employees only. In past years, the large electronic outlet where Fred worked had made it a point to include spouses and significant others at the holiday celebration. So it was a big surprise to Dana when she learned she was not invited.

At Dana's first visit, she explained that she and Fred had been married for seven years. They had one child, with one on the way (which was quite evident by Dana's appearance). She went over the details about Fred's office hours and where he was expected to be during the Christmas party. It was obvious she was in emotional pain.

She said the party was being held on a cruise ship, but didn't know which one. She said it included a tour around San Francisco Bay, past Angel Island, San Francisco, Sausalito, and the Berkeley Marina.

I knew Ann and I had a difficult assignment on our hands. First, company parties tend to be private, with the entire yacht being booked for a certain time period. Secondly, there are several cruise ships around the Bay providing this same holiday activity. And last, but not least, how were we to get on Fred's particular cruise ship?

We began calling the various cruise lines. We called Red & White, Blue & Gold ... you name it across the color spectrum. Finally, Ann reached the Hornblower, and the agent informed her that "our party" was leaving Berkeley on the evening of December 3rd. Boarding time was 7:30 p.m., and departure was at 8 o'clock sharp.

Ann came up with an excellent idea on how we could get aboard without being spotted. She suggested we approach the captain of the Hornblower at least thirty minutes before departure and inform him we were two undercover investigators working on a possible drug buy. We'd tell him it was supposed to take place that night on his charter and, due to confidentiality; we couldn't inform him who the suspect was. To assuage any anxieties on the captain's part, we would assure him that it was quite possible this individual was innocent.

I thought the idea was brilliant! On the night of the party, we approached the captain with our story. He was more than helpful, and even asked what he could do to assist us. To help us blend into the crowd, Ann had rented a French maid's outfit that had a low-cut white ruffle blouse and short skirt. She wore black nylons with a seam going up the back. I wore a Naval Officer's uniform—with egg yolk and all. The Captain and I stood on the ramp greeting the passengers as they embarked, and Ann went to the kitchen to get things set up for us. After everyone was aboard, I strolled among the passengers with the video camera, pretending to videotape everyone while they were dancing and having fun.

"Freddie," as I called him, wasn't difficult to find. He was enjoying the company of a petite, south-of-the-border beauty, dancing and generally making an ass out of himself. He reminded me of Jim Carey in the movie, "Mask." This guy even had the balls to sing a couple of songs from the seventies—off key, no less. It was difficult not to laugh out loud.

Between dances, Freddie and his little "cha-cha" were obviously enjoying each other's company. Lots of handholding, adoring glances, feeding each other prawns dipped in cocktail sauce ... the body language of lovers. And "Admiral Clouthier" was taping every bit of it.

The cruise lasted until 11:00 p.m. Freddie was obviously liquored up, so his date had to drive them to her place in Oakland. We followed them and waited outside until 1:00 a.m. It was apparent that Freddie was staying the night.

We had promised Dana we would call her before we ended our surveillance. I hated calling so late, knowing she needed all the sleep she could get, but I suspected she wasn't asleep anyway. The phone rang only once before Dana answered.

"Hello?"

"Dana, this is Greg. How are you feeling?"

"Okay ... but somehow I don't think I'll be feeling very good in a minute from now."

"You're pretty intuitive, aren't you?"

"Just answer me this: Is he sleeping with her?"

"I'll just tell you that the lights went out at her place around midnight and they haven't been seen since. Does that answer your question?"

"Yes, it sure does. When can I see the film?"

"Would tomorrow be soon enough?"

"That's fine. I'll call you tomorrow morning to arrange a time."

"Good night, Dana."

Ann felt sorry for Dana and wondered if there were any comforting words of wisdom we could provide. I told her not to worry too much, that Dana seemed to be stronger than she looked. I pointed out that during our interview and conversations she never once got teary-eyed. Then I laughed as I thought about the videotape. It would probably bring a tear or two ... most likely tears of laughter!

Dana called late the next morning and made arrangements for our meeting. We brought a portable video monitor that plays our 8mm videotapes. I was right about Dana. After the initial shock, she laughed all the way through the videotape. At the end of the film when Freddie was seen entering his lover's apartment, Dana's only comment was, "Well that's that." Ann asked Dana what her plans were and Dana replied that she would be moving back to San Francisco to be near her mother. "But first, I'm going to have this baby on Freddie's medical plan. And then I'll leave him."

"Are you going to confront him?" Ann asked.

"No! I'm just going to wait it out, get my ducks in a row, and then leave him."

She smiled wickedly as she added, "I think I'll leave him a copy of this videotape too!"

7

The Electronic Arsenal

Charlotte was a sweet young mother of adorable daughters, ages 3 and 4. A third child was on the way, due to arrive in about two months. She and Clay had been married for eight years. It was her first marriage and Clay's second. He had previously married at 19, divorced at 26, and then had several off-and-on relationships until he met Charlotte. She was 19 when they first started dating. They had an intense relationship and married within the year. During the first five years the young couple struggled, but their marriage was loving and fulfilling. The problems began when Clay accepted a business opportunity in California's Silicon Valley, heartland of the computer industry and birthplace of the microchip.

Clay and Charlotte packed up their worldly belongings and moved from Revere, Massachusetts, to the Golden State, hoping to strike it rich. And they did, thanks to Clay's long hours. Within three short years, they bought a beautiful home in the exclusive Bay Area bedroom community of Alamo. The old Chevy was traded in for a BMW with all the bells and whistles, and everything seemed perfect. But now we sit at Scott's, a fashionable seafood restaurant, this adorable, very pregnant, 28-year old and I. Tears are running down her sweet cheeks and people are looking at me as though I'm the villain.

"What makes you think he's having an affair?" I ask.

"Well," whispers Charlotte between sobs, "first of all, he's spending far too much time at work. Plus, I've seen his American Express and Visa credit card receipts and they show dinners for two, motel bills for double occupancy. Need I go on?"

"No. It sounds like you have a legitimate reason to suspect your husband is having an affair. Is there anything he says that makes you suspect that he's seeing another woman?"

"He tells me to keep out of his personal finances and says he doesn't need to explain anything to me."

"Have there been any other signs of infidelity," I ask, "like weight loss, petty arguments, joining a health club, phone calls all hours of the night when he isn't home?" Each symptom causes Charlotte to wince. "Oh my God!" is all she can mumble.

"About a year ago, when I first suspected he was seeing someone, he had lost about thirty pounds, was coming home late, and would start stupid little arguments over absolutely nothing. Then the phone calls started. Just about 15 or 20 minutes before he got home, the phone would ring and wake me up. I would say 'hello' repeatedly, but there was just silence on the other end of the line and then they would hang up."

"Charlotte, if we do find that Clay is cheating, do you have an action plan?"

"Well, it'll depend on how he treats me. I like California, but I'd move back to Massachusetts in a second to be with my family if he didn't want to save our marriage. Whenever I try to talk to him about my feelings and concerns, he just tells me I'm imagining things. He laughs it off, saying it's just hormones and watching too many soaps."

"Let's see what I can do to reassure you one way or the other. First, do you have any idea who he may be seeing and where?"

"I think its Mariette. I overheard him calling the office one morning and raising his voice. He said her name like he was annoyed, and then he saw me standing at the door and turned his back on me, whispered something, and hung up. Then he accused me of spying on him. I'm sure its Mariette. She's married and her last name is Bondur. I've seen her at company dinners and picnics, and she's the flirty type. She also gives me "the look," as if she knows something I don't."

The next day, one of my agents, Tracy, sets up surveillance off the Bayshore Highway in Burlingame, just down the street from Clay's office. Clay is expected to arrive around 8:00 a.m., and he does, wearing a three-piece blue suit and carrying a briefcase.

The hours go by slowly. Tracy has to keep changing his surveillance site because of too many suspicious bystanders, but he's able to find a location where he can still keep an eye on the office and Clay's car. The noon hour comes and goes. Clay never leaves the office.

Finally, Tracy contacts me and I report to Charlotte, telling her that nothing is happening. Charlotte says it isn't unusual for Clay to stay in for lunch, but he would definitely go out for dinner. I notify Tracy and assure him I'll be nearby well before the close of business.

I arrive just before 4:30 p.m., and Clay's BMW is still parked where Tracy had said it would be. I park where Tracy had been earlier in the day and am able to easily follow Clay when he leaves the office at 6:23 p.m., driving directly to a nearby gas station. Tracy and I can't pull in directly behind him without causing some suspicion, so I pass the station and radio back to Tracy to stop and ask for directions while I turn around. When I return to the station, I don't see Tracy, Clay, or his BMW. I get on the freeway and head north, which is the way Clay would travel if he were going home. I call Charlotte on my cell phone to see if Clay has called her. She says she hasn't heard from him all day and is holding dinner for him. I tell her what has happened, and that I'll attempt to reach Tracy by radio to see where they are.

I pull off the freeway at Foster City and contact Tracy. He's just a few blocks ahead of me, sitting at a gas station just outside a gated apartment complex. It seems Clay is inside, and we need to figure out how to get in there after him.

We don't need to drive both cars in, so Tracy parks his car and joins me. We drive up to the security officer; I flash my credentials and ask nicely if he will let us in. The gate opens. We quickly locate Clay's car parked in the garage, and we know there's no way of catching him in a compromising position tonight.

I call Charlotte and tell her what's happened, but she doesn't seem disappointed. She comments they're getting together with a marriage counselor on Tuesday morning and perhaps we could follow Clay and monitor his cell phone. I agree, and Tracy and I call it a night.

On Tuesday morning Tracy mans our newest toy—the cellular scanner—as we perch outside the Danville office of Clay and Charlotte's marriage counselor. Charlotte and Clay emerge from the office and get into their respective cars. We overhear Charlotte asking her husband to drive safely and have a good day, which she backs up with a gentle kiss on the cheek. Clay settles himself into the soft leather upholstery of his BMW, waves good-bye to his wife, and drives towards the southbound ramp to the 680 freeway. Charlotte follows. A traffic light stops Clay and he uses the cell phone to dial his message center.

Our nifty little scanner picked up the radio waves for the number we had programmed it to search for, displayed the number being dialed, and then recorded the conversation. We were also able to learn his access code when he entered it to retrieve his messages. There were three calls. The first call had been at 7:20 a.m. today; "Hi, Clay. Call me this morning at home before 8:00, or at the office if it's after. Love you!"

Clay doesn't wait to hear the rest of his messages. He immediately dials his office. "Mari! Hi Baby! Got your message." At the precise point that Clay puts the phone to his ear, his lovely pregnant wife stops next to him at the red light, rolls down the window, and shouts, "I love you!"

We're located several cars behind them, but our recorder is able to pick up everything. Clay tells Mariette to hang on for a moment, rolls down his window, barely covers the mouthpiece, and shouts back, "I love you too, Honey."

Charlotte then turns to the left as Clay turns to the right. We next hear Mariette asking, "Who was that?"

"Oh, that's the ball and chain. We just left the shrink. I fed the idiot a bunch of garbage about how Charlotte and I are growing further apart and don't communicate like we used to. Charlotte even accused me of having an affair, but I convinced them both that it's just Charlotte's overactive imagination and the pregnancy, and that I'm just working extra hard to get the business off the ground. "Stupid" and "the fat girl" believed me."

We taped the laughter from both ends of the conversation.

Mariette's next question: "Honey, when are you going to send her packing?"

"Not too long now, Baby. Hey, what are you wearing today?"

"I'm wearing my black short skirt and an emerald green sweater with a lacy blouse underneath, high heels and, just for you, no panties."

"Ummm, I can't wait to get to the office."

"Well," Mariette continues to tease him, "while you're having the meeting this afternoon, you can think of me and what we can do after work. By the way, I bought some nice towels for the bathroom, and some new linens. We really need to fix our place up if we're ever going to move in together."

"Yeah, you're probably right. Does your husband suspect anything yet?"

"Not him! He wouldn't know I was fooling around even if it happened in his own bed. He's such a klutz! We had a real big fight last night about why I don't fuck him. I told him that's all he ever thinks of me for—just for fucking. I'll never touch that idiot ever again. Are you being faithful to me?"

"Are you kidding? Have you seen her? She's huge! No way, Honey. She repulses me. I'll see you and that short skirt in about 30 minutes. Bye!"

Tracy disconnects the record button.

Charlotte had previously provided us with the names of all the women in Clay's office, married or not. There was only one Mariette Bondur, and she was married to Peter Hughes.

I met with Charlotte later that afternoon so she could listen to the tape. It was heart wrenching, but I could tell a tremendous burden had been lifted. She kept our little secret until the next meeting with the marriage counselor a few days later. When Clay began his usual denial of any affair, Charlotte, feeling safe in the therapist's office, let Clay hear the recording.

Their next meeting was with an attorney. The two of them were able to reach an agreement on visitation rights; Clay could see his kids several times a year in Massachusetts. The two sides also managed to hammer out an equitable settlement, which included very generous support payments to Charlotte. In the end, Charlotte's powerful, insider husband didn't have as much of the high ground as she thought. It seems Clay's business partners would not have been pleased with his after-hours behavior, so Clay was ready to accommodate any reasonable request for the assurance the story wouldn't get back to the executive washroom.

8

Cheating?
Or Not?

Men who embark on extramarital affairs usually try to keep them secret. They don't want to give up on their marriages. Not just yet ... if at all. Still, their attempts at secrecy are often flawed, sometimes ridiculously so.

This was vividly demonstrated in the case of Inga and her cheating husband.

I was at my office when the phone rang. The woman's voice sounded Germanic, and she was definitely tense.

"Please, I vant some help mit mine husband. I tink he deceives me," she said.

I asked her to explain.

"He begins to argue mit me over nothing. I don't like to fight and I don't understand. I do not spend too much. The

house looks goot. Our children are goot children. Vhy is he being so angry?"

She had good reason to ask. A new pattern of constant fighting is definitely a danger signal, and I asked my caller to tell me more. She identified herself as Inga and said she was from Berlin. Her American husband, Matt, was a high-powered contractor whose work on Bay Area real estate developments took him to new locations nearly every day. In the past, he would always let her know where he could be reached. Now she would call him, only to find he wasn't where he said he would be.

"Sometimes at the job site they say he hasn't been there all day!"

Also, he was coming home late, 6:30 or 7:00 instead of his usual 5:00. Inga noticed the late days were when the arguments generally occurred. Furthermore, his wardrobe had changed.

"My husband, normally he doesn't dress up for his work; casual shirts, jeans, and boots. The job site can be very dirty, you know. But now," she added sadly, "he becomes stylish. You must see these clothes. Just like the Wild West cowboy movies. Matt has fancy shirts, the best denim jeans and boots … six pairs of them! Some are made of the leather of lizards."

I stifled a laugh. I'd never heard alligator boots referred to in this way. But it let me know she was observant, and that she was onto something.

"Okay, I'll take the case," I said. "Meet me Monday morning at 9:30," and I gave her my office address.

Inga was right on time. She looked to be about 40, tall, and well dressed in a tailored blue wool dress that subtly accented her athletic figure. Tasteful makeup and jewelry completed her outfit. It's important to notice these things. I want to know if a man is cheating because his wife has let herself go or for some other reason. Also, if there's a big gap between what he's earning and what she's wearing, that can be a clue.

After handing her some coffee to break the ice, I started. "You told me some reasons you think Matt is cheating. Are there others?"

"Oh, *ya,*" Inga said, "I've been thinking about it ever since we spoke." She had noticed that in addition to his new clothes, changed schedule, and quarrelsomeness, he had started taking more care with his grooming. "Usually he is good-looking, but sloppy. You are similar, I think."

I squirmed as I realized the truth of her comments.

"These days, Matt sometimes puts on nice cologne to go to work. His hair is more, how you say, neat. And he even loses a few pounds."

"How is he doing that?" I asked, although I had a feeling I already knew.

"He is not dieting. Matt, he likes cheeseburgers better than anything. But let me show you how he has changed."

And she pulled out a manila envelope.

Aha! The evidence ... my favorite thing. Photos, a list of their vehicles (Mercedes 560 coupe, Rolls Royce sedan, and Toyota pickup truck), Matt's business address, and the name and address of the woman Inga suspected of being the lover. The photo of Matt showed a big, rugged-looking man with a full head of brown hair and maybe 25 pounds of too many cheeseburgers around the waist.

"This was last year," said Inga sharply. "Now he doesn't have the fat stomach."

I asked how old he was, and found he was 43. Yep, right on schedule. "Is there any more evidence?"

"The phone calls," she said flatly, staring at me. "That is what convinces me." Their phone at home would ring. Inga would answer and hear breathing at the other end. After a few seconds, the caller would hang up. This was happening four or five times a week, usually coinciding with the days Matt was absent from work. Inga then gave me the clincher.

"Matt had affair two years ago. He says it is over."

Well, maybe it was and maybe it wasn't. A man who has cheated once has broken the taboo barrier. Once he survives being caught, he often does it again ... sometimes with the same partner. He conveniently forgets the painful scenes from when he was caught the first time.

The recent changes in Matt's life added up to one thing. He probably was cheating again. Inga's husband had given off a multitude of the classic danger signals. Inga asked me to follow Matt for a week, around-the-clock. I said it would cost less if we followed the other woman, but she insisted. I agreed to tail him, take photographs and video, and submit a report. She gave me a retainer and left with a regretful sigh. This had been a painful, but necessary, decision for her.

My wife, Ann, and I picked up the trail the next morning. Matt was a reckless driver, aggressively changing lanes, running red lights and speeding. It was tough to follow him. It wasn't like he suspected anything; he just drove like a maniac. After two days, we gave up and decided to focus on the other woman. We would stake her out and let Matt come to us.

We found out that Lisa, the woman Inga suspected, was married. She worked as a loan officer at a bank where Matt's contracting company had an account. She appeared to be about 30, red-haired, with a decent figure, but she didn't pay much attention to her appearance. We watched her for about a week, and every day she would emerge from work in a baggy outfit, her hair trailing in the wind, no makeup, and a harried expression.

Then Thursday afternoon arrived. At first, we weren't even sure it was the same person. She was sporting a stylish hair-do, makeup, push-up bra, a red knit dress, and—probably—a garter belt under that clingy skirt. Beyond the flattering dress and makeup, she also had that indescribable air about her that catches a man's eye. She reminded me of those before-and-after makeovers.

"Bingo," I said to myself. "Today's the day."

We tracked her to the Marina Vista Hotel, a quality place at San Francisco's Fisherman's Wharf. As she got out of her car to go inside, I caught the glint in her eye. Since Lisa was mimicking Matt and was doing just what cheating husbands do—giving her best to someone else—I didn't feel too sorry for her as I got out my camera to videotape her meeting my client's husband. She walked into the lobby of the hotel, then reappeared and walked up the outside stairs to Room 208. About fifteen minutes later, Matt drove up and parked. We filmed him as he went to the hotel office and then came out to follow the same route Lisa had taken.

For two hours Ann and I waited in the van, parked five feet from Lisa's bronze Mustang. We made small talk and kept our cameras ready. At 6:12 p.m., Matt and Lisa came out of the hotel together. Whatever discretion they had shown before was gone now. They didn't try to hide a thing. Matt escorted her to her car and passionately kissed her goodbye.

You'd think that after two hours, he would have had enough, but I've noticed that cheating husbands like to leave some sort of territorial marking on the woman they've just romanced. They take all sorts of precautions beforehand to keep their love trails secret, but once the act is done they seem compelled to show off to the public. It's stupid because it gives indisputable proof of their philandering. And Matt, like so many others, was going to pay for his folly.

Sure enough! Right in front of our camera Matt pinned Lisa up against her car for one final clinch and groin rubbing. What great evidence! Finally, they pried themselves apart. He gave her a final pat on her behind and left.

The next morning I showed the video to Inga. I never know how to feel during these meetings. On the one hand, I've gotten what my client wanted: the hard evidence. On the other hand, the client isn't really very happy about getting it. It's one thing to say, "bring me proof," but another thing to watch your husband pawing another woman. Inga let out a few choice comments in her native language, but stayed in control. Later I found out how she cleverly got her revenge.

During the next few months, Inga would stop Matt just as he was rushing out the door. She would hand him a stack of papers to sign, telling him they were routine transactions—car registration renewals or credit card payments. Secretly, she was mixing in documents that signed over the title to the house, the expensive cars, and the bank accounts to her. Then she bought a copy of Matt's favorite movie, *"The Great Escape,"* and took it to an electronics expert who spliced the videotape I had given her into the middle of the movie.

A few nights later, she fixed Matt's favorite meal. After dessert she said, "Matt, I have a question to ask you. Have you ever been unfaithful to me since that affair two years ago?"

Matt let out the groan of the imposed-upon, falsely accused innocent. "I can't believe you're still dragging up that old thing," he complained. "One time I mess up—ONE TIME—and you can't let it go."

This is a common practice of cheating husbands. They moan and groan and play innocent, trying to make their wives think they're crazy for being suspicious.

"All right," she said quietly. "I'll never ask you again." She then suggested they watch *"The Great Escape."* Settling down in their easy chairs, they watched as the allied prisoners of war ingeniously outwitted their German captors. When they got to the scene where Steve McQueen is put back into solitary confinement, the front door of Inga's home silently opened. A police officer and a process server slipped in behind Matt. It was at that very moment, just as Inga had timed it, that the videotaped scene of Matt's rendezvous appeared on the screen.

Inga watched in delight as Matt stared at the TV. His jaw dropped and the popcorn literally fell out of his mouth.

"I ... uh ... I," he stuttered.

The process server quickly stepped forward, handed Matt a piece of paper, and simply stated, "You are being sued for divorce."

The policeman then escorted him out of the house to the garage, where Inga had placed his already-packed suitcases. In less than five minutes, he had gone from being a happy, well-off, two-timing businessman to a pauper with two suitcases and a pickup truck.

Inga's careful planning had paid off. She ended up with a handsome settlement and possession of an 18-room home in an exclusive San Francisco Bay Area community. More importantly, she was able to regain the confidence her husband had all but shattered in pursuit of cheap thrills. Dating again and feeling good about herself, She came out on top.

9

With Two You Get Egg Roll

Dr. Philip Benjamin was a prominent pediatrician who was adored by his young patients as well as their parents. His wise, comforting manner and genuine concern for their welfare easily won the hearts of all who turned to him for medical care. He was also a solid pillar of the community. As a member of several civic groups, he could always be counted on to make handsome donations to worthwhile causes. Since Dr. Benjamin and his wife, Diane, had no children of their own, people assumed his philanthropy and kindly manner were his way of sharing his love for the children he didn't have.

Philip and Diane lived in an elegant home where they often entertained other well-to-do professionals. One of the centerpieces of the home was Philip's twelve-foot aquarium full of rare tropical fish and eels. It was an aquatic treasure worth at least $35,000. Prominently featured in his den, the tropical creatures lived in a dramatically illuminated underwater wonderland of ceramic castles, miniature reefs, and even little kelp forests. Each of the brightly colored fish had fancy names like "Tinker Bell," "Duchess," and "Heather," while the eels were given villainous names like "Lobo" and "Hulk."

Whenever Philip was at home, the fish were his companions. He would sit in front of the tank and happily watch them for hours, dropping little treats into the water and watching them scurry upward to grab them. It made a touching scene, and certainly showed how sensitive this kind and gentle man was to the world's smaller creatures.

But there was much more to Dr. Benjamin, which I was soon to learn.

On the advice of a friend, Diane Benjamin called me one day. She was quite sure this well-liked pillar of the community was cheating on her. She had several clues; but of course whenever she confronted him he always denied everything, and made her feel like a witch for even suggesting such a thing.

As we talked it soon became very clear that Dr. Benjamin was not the same man everyone admired and respected. In fact, the stories she told me of his unkindness still make me wince. Behind closed doors, she said Philip was abusive, contemptuous, miserly, and mean. For years he had withheld from her the love that he showered on strangers. He especially reveled in humiliating her in front of waiters and other people who served the public. Birthdays and anniversaries passed by without any kind of acknowledgement, however Philip never failed to point out any mistakes she made in arranging their social life or managing the home. Only the fish received his undivided attention. (I couldn't help but wonder if this was his opportunity to play God—creating his own little world that he could rule without any back talk. He reminded me of Dr. No, the enemy of James Bond, who was another gentleman with a fish fetish.) Diane also shared with me that Philip had quite a temper and had hit her on more than one occasion. Like many women, she had swallowed her shock and hoped it would never happen again.

Diane described Philip as short, dumpy, and balding, and she commented that she couldn't see what women found attractive about him. I ignored her remark because I have learned that such men can find lovers as easily as the handsome ones—especially if they have money or power.

I told Diane I would find out if her suspicions were correct. A few days later, Mark, my assistant, and I staked out the good doctor's office. I was in my Mercedes Benz and Mark was in a plain-looking surveillance van. After a few hours, we saw him leave the office in his silver Mercedes sedan and followed him to the parking lot of a local steakhouse in San Mateo. We discreetly parked at a distance.

Just after 2 o'clock, a green Volvo station wagon pulled up next to him. A wholesome-looking brunette, appearing to be in her mid-20's, was the driver. We watched as Philip got into the young lady's Volvo.

Mark started up the van and pulled into the parking lot, casually backing it up to the Volvo where he could train the surveillance camera in the rear of the van on the action. The two acted like horny teenagers who had sneaked out of the house to make out in the back of a car, which was visibly vibrating with their lovemaking. Some of the people coming out of the restaurant walked right by, while others actually peeked in! In either case, our Romeo and Juliet were oblivious.

I found it interesting that, although the doctor could easily have afforded the best hotel in town, he preferred the back seat of a car. Maybe that was part of the thrill—pretending this was a 1959 Thunderbird and that he was again, if ever, the red-hot, irresistible lover. Well, this adventure had one thing in common with teenage groupies: he was defying someone.

Mark and I spent two afternoons and one evening in this same parking lot videotaping the restaurant romance—the arrivals, prolonged car visits, and clinging good-byes. When we finally showed Diane the tape, she said with some bitterness, "And this is the man I put through medical school! Where would he be if I hadn't worked as a secretary for eight years? I helped to make him the success he is today!"

It was apparent that she was hurt and angry, and with good reason. After reviewing the evidence, I couldn't help but admire Diane when she told me she wasn't about to let this pompous, philandering doctor off lightly. She had already begun masterminding a scene that would make Lucrezia Borgia proud. Her trap would accomplish three things: he'd be forced out of the house, she would have incontrovertible testimony she could use in the divorce proceedings, and she would have her sweet moment of revenge. She was going to hang him by the balls.

She asked me to help her collect some financial data from her husband's office. She had a duplicate set of keys, so one evening when she was sure he would be busy, we went to his office. Diane found what she was looking for and we left.

Shortly thereafter, Diane put together a fancy dinner party. She invited a few distinguished guests that included a judge and the district attorney. She told Philip to expect his favorite dish, which she served to great applause. Afterwards, Philip escorted everyone into his private den to admire his aquarium. After seating his guests, he dimmed the room lights and switched on the multicolored aquarium lights.

Everyone watched as the kelp flowed gently back and forth and the bubbles floated lazily to the surface from the aquarium floor. They patiently waited for the exotic Who's Who of Tropical Fish to fill the aquarium with their brilliant colors. Mysteriously, no fish appeared. The aquarium looked empty. Several moments passed and the silence grew awkward. Phil looked perplexed, then worried.

"Where are my fish?" he frantically asked.

Diane, who had been standing in the doorway, savoring the moment, gave him her most angelic smile and said, "How'd you like your stir-fry?"

After an appalled instant, he realized what she had done. With a gasp and a roar, he hurled himself across the room and attacked her in full view of the horrified guests. Totally out of control with rage, he chased her like a homicidal maniac down the hallways, shrieking and cursing at her, "You killed my fucking fish!"

Doors slammed. Diane screamed. The guests were in complete shock as they watched this dignified, highly respected pillar of the community go berserk. Then, as if in a high-class farce, the warring parties careened through the doorway, Diane in front, Philip in hot pursuit—the expensively gowned woman and the bellowing bullock. Along the way, Diane had lost her shoes and some of her jewelry. Her face was flushed and taut with fear.

Finally, after circling the tables and chairs a couple of times, Philip caught up with her. He threw her to the ground and began pummeling her. Even the most etiquette-conscious guest realized it was time to take action, and the men in the party lunged forward to pull Philip away while the women immediately encircled Diane protectively. Once things had died down a little, the police were called and the party broke up in disarray.

Later that week, Diane began divorce proceedings. Backed up by unimpeachable witnesses who would swear to the all-too-public act of violence by the esteemed Dr. Philip Benjamin, Diane won a handsome settlement in addition to her revenge, which, as she put it, was all too delicious.

Even in today's age of equality, many women are still brought up thinking they are expected to make sacrifices for their man, let him take all the credit and wield the power, and to suffer silently if or when they are mistreated. And for many, it was drummed into them that they had no recourse. Even after seeing other women get out of bad marriages and start new lives, plenty of women simply can't imagine it for themselves. Nor can they find the words to protest the power imbalance.

Therefore, they quietly cheer the woman who triumphs and they revel in the man's loss of everything he has hoarded—money, prestige, and power. It's only human nature to relish the oppressor's downfall after being treated like a second-class citizen for decades.

If you recognize yourself in this portrait of a woman who has let herself be devalued, there's a lot to learn from Diane's story. It's not easy to escape your conditioning, but if you've been suffering indignities for years, just remember it's never too late.

But that's another book.

Another point I would like to make is that if you are someone who is looking for a new mate, keep in mind that the

most upstanding man in town could be hiding a secret life—
one that may shock you. Gambling, infidelity, drugs, even
child abuse, may sully the lives of those who are admired in
the community. My psychologist friends tell me it's not really all that mysterious, that a man's public virtue is his way of
trying to get away from the miserable self he acts out pri-
vately. The more his dark side shows at home, the more he
reassures himself by putting on a halo in public.

I must also issue a warning. Please don't take Diane's tale
as a license to play Rambo; you could get hurt. When a man
is humiliated and cornered, he can strike out violently, even
kill. A lot of the stories you hear in the news about a so-called
upstanding citizen suddenly shooting his family are often
about a marital partner that has been driven to the point of
desperation. This is especially so if the law has helped the
more powerful partner and left the other feeling completely
victimized.

And there's one more thing to consider: some fish are not
edible and are downright poisonous. Diane was fortunate that
no one was harmed. She would have been wiser to sell the
fish to a collector or flushed them, whatever felt best, and
then put a stir-fry together consisting of a medley of the local
fish market's catch of the day. Just let the good doctor think
he'd digested his little darlings!

10

For Whom
The Del Tolls

I received a call from a very distraught young woman on
Thursday, December 14, wanting to meet with me right
away at the Starbuck's in Walnut Creek. Upon arrival I
noticed a young woman in her late twenties with shoulder
length brown hair sitting outside with an infant in a convertible car seat carrier. I was hoping this wasn't Carol, but as
luck would have it, it was. Carol had only been home from
the hospital a few days after delivering her second child. She
was meeting with me because she needed to have her husband of six years followed to San Diego. It was his birthday
bash, and Carol wasn't invited to join in the festivities.

"Is this normal for your husband to leave you behind on
his birthday?"

"No," Carol replied.

"Then why now?" I asked.

"When our first child was born, I caught him cheating on me. It all started to go bad between us when I became pregnant. Now here I am again, feeling suspicious of my husband's activities. He didn't even drive me to the hospital this time, and he only visited me once in three days. He told me that he was very busy at work! Charles was like this when our first child was born, too. Can you check out his flight tomorrow from Oakland to San Diego? He's flying on Southwest, leaving at 8:05 p.m. and arriving at 9:30."

I replied that I could, but that it would be even easier if Carol did this herself. I told her to call Southwest and confirm his reservation for "two" to San Diego, instructing her not to put her inquiry in the form of a question, and see what they say.

"Just call and say you forgot the departure time and want to be sure to be there in time for preflight loading and security checks. Then give them your husband's name. They will usually confirm his take off and arrival times with you; and, of course this way you don't have to pay us for finding information that you can do yourself. Be sure to do this today in case you want us to do anything in San Diego for you tomorrow."

"Good idea! I'll call you later this afternoon to tell you what I found out and we can decide if I'll need your assistance in San Diego."

Within an hour Carol called me back, her voice cracking. I could imagine her big brown eyes and the tears flowing down her rounded cheeks as she tried to get the words out. "His reservations are confirmed with Karen Kyle, my very best friend since childhood. Oh God ... Oh God ... I just can't believe this!" I tried to calm her down, but I don't think she heard my voice. I truly hate these moments. If only her husband could see the pain she was suffering. "Can you fly down there with an agent and get photos or something for me?"

"Let me confirm it with my agent, and I will get back with you today."

I called my partner, Ann—who just also happens to be my wife—and asked if she could accompany me to San Diego in the morning for a surveillance that would last a few days. Ann agreed, and I informed Ann of the situation: that Carol's best friend was flying down to San Diego with Carol's husband and staying at The Hotel del Coronado while Carol stayed home with her days-old infant daughter and two-year-old son. After hearing a few descriptive phrases about Carol's husband such as "pond scum" and "worm," I knew Ann was as anxious as I was to make the worm squirm. I called Southwest and made reservations for two to arrive in San Diego twelve hours before Charles and Carol's former best friend were scheduled to arrive.

We checked into our room in the old and very quaint Victorian part of the hotel, with a partial view of Pt. Loma lighthouse, the majestic cliffs, and dark blue ocean. Staying at The Del is a treat by most everyone's standards; I remembered Carol telling me they were always trying to save money when they traveled, and stayed at far less expensive hotel chains. While I chewed on that, Ann went down to the lobby and asked if her friends, the Clarks, had arrived. The desk clerk told Ann that the Clarks were scheduled to arrive in the late evening and asked if Ann would like to leave a message for them.

"No, thank you."

With that piece of information, we could accomplish a lot in the meantime. I called Carol to tell her that we had arrived at The Del, gave her our room number and phone number,

and told her to feel free to check in with us from time to time
to get the latest updates. I had asked Carol for a physical
description of Karen and also learned that Karen was married
with one child.

Carol asked, "How long do you think it will take to catch
them?"

"Who knows? We can only wait and hope for the best. But
the fact that we're all staying in the same hotel is a big help."

Ann and I had a late dinner at the popular Mexican
restaurant up the street and returned to The Del's main
lobby by 9 o'clock. Then we sat back and watched the registration desk while we nibbled from a fruit and cheese platter. Within an hour Charles and Karen walked up the entry-
way stairs, hand-in-hand, to the reservation desk. I had
placed the video camera around the corner of the massive
front desk while Ann took up her position in line behind
Karen. While waiting their turn to check in, Karen was
showing off to Ann by patting Charles' rear and nibbling on
his ear. When the cashier announced their room number,
Ann stepped forward to hear: "Room 6424." This was a room
in the new, modern building, away from the rustic main
building. Charles, Karen, Ann, and I headed outside and
down the pathway. Ann and I acted as though we were a bit
lost and fumbled for our key, the whole time staying close
enough to see Charles and Karen enter their room. Ann and
I immediately headed for the stairs and went outside to the
walkway by the beach and swaying palm trees. We looked up
at the hotel and immediately noticed Charles and Karen on
the balcony in a tender embrace. I held my camera up and
captured the whole twenty minutes of passionate kisses and
embraces. This would certainly be enough to convince Carol
of Charles' "indescretion."

Ann and I returned to our room and called Carol, who was surprisingly calm and seemed pleased that we had been able to provide the evidence so quickly. I told Carol that Ann and I would check out of the hotel and fly home in the morning.

"No! I want you to keep an eye on them all day tomorrow until I arrive there with my mom. It should take me all day to drive down there, but I'll start packing things up now. I'll call you tomorrow."

All of the next day we kept our distance and watched the lovers shop and eat in nearby La Jolla, awaiting Carol's arrival. At 7:30, Carol was at our door; but instead of her mother, she had brought along her father and brother. After making the introductions, she sat down on the edge of the bed and I plugged my videotape into the TV. Tears flowed as Carol watched the video of Charles and Karen on the balcony. Her father gently patted her on the back and whispered, "It'll be OK, Honey." Her brother placed his hand on her shoulder and told her that she would always be loved, and her family would always be by her side. I couldn't help but think that if more of my clients could have their family's support during these stressful times, it would be so much easier for the victims of infidelity. They usually feel so alone, ashamed and responsible.

Carol's tears dried up, and she even managed a smile as she asked if we knew where Charles and Karen were at the moment. Since Karen and Charles were last seen shopping, and would now likely be enjoying a romantic dinner, we guessed that they would come wandering back to the hotel by ten o'clock. We decided to go to a Marie Calendar's a few blocks away to grab a quick supper and plan our strategy for the evening. But first I asked Ann to take Carol to the lobby to get a key to "her" room.

Ann took Carol down to the lobby while Carol's brother and I watched the stairway and main entrance. Carol approached the young woman at the front desk and introduced herself. "My name is Carol Clark. I've locked myself out of my room, Room 6424, may I have another key?"

"May I see an ID?"

Carol reached into her wallet and produced her driver's license, and the clerk then handed Carol the keycard. Carol's family, Ann, and I drove up Orange Avenue, enjoyed a nice meal, and discussed the misery we planned to bring to bear on the unsuspecting and very deserving couple in Room 6424.

Afterwards Carol, her father and brother returned to our room while Ann and I stayed downstairs in our rental car to await the arrival of Charles and Karen. The minute we spotted them and saw them wander towards the building where their room was, I called Carol. Thanks to the large glass doors and windows of the lobby, we could see them getting in the elevator. Ann went with them in the elevator, but just stayed in the elevator as if she was going to a higher floor.

When the coast was clear, Ann returned to the car and confirmed that the twosome went directly to their room. I called Carol and told her, "It's time!" Stan, Carol's father, was instructed to get their car and pull it in front of the new wing, with the engine running and the car door open. Ann, Carol, her brother Jason, and I took the elevator to the fourth floor. Ann stayed behind at the elevator to make sure that the elevator stayed on the fourth floor, no matter what.

Carol, Jason, and I headed right to Room 6424. I walked up to the door and listened. The undeniable rhythmic sound of a bed squeaking told me that this would be the perfect moment. I whispered to Carol, "Are you ready?"

"You bet I am."

Jason had wanted to go with Carol to protect her, but I insisted that he stay in the hallway with me. "I don't want this to get out of control. I'll videotape this "visit" from just outside the door, and we won't say a word." If Charles should try to attack Carol, then we would step in. Thankfully Jason, like his father, accepted my directions without an argument.

Carol pulled out one of those "throw-away" cameras and declared, I'm ready!" With that, she slipped the keycard in the door and barged into the room. The sound of the squeaking bed abruptly stopped, followed by a muffled scream of surprise, and a masculine voice shouting, "What the hell?" I saw the image of Carol in my viewfinder.

"Hi, assholes!"

A flash when off, and the room was flooded ever so briefly in white light. Carol was standing at the foot of the bed, yelling every profanity she could think of to show her displeasure at what she was witnessing. While Carol yelled, I notice the bedspread slowly being pulled up to cover their nakedness. Suddenly, Carol stopped berating them, placed the camera at her feet, and tugged the blankets and sheets from Charles' grasp. Carol reached down in the darkness and picked up the camera again and said, "This one's for your husband, you bitch! You'll never know the day I'll send these pictures to your husband!"

After that last flash of light, Carol walked out the door and slammed it so hard that it literally shook the entire building. Jason, Carol and I flew around the corner to find Ann holding the elevator for us. When we reached the ground floor, Carol and Jason jumped into the waiting car and sped off. Ann and I walked up to our rental car and watched the door to see what Charles would do. He broke a record in getting his shorts on and getting down four flights to the parking lot, calling out, and jumping up and down trying to spot her among the rows of parked cars. "Carol, Carol I ... Carol, Honey, Carol, Carol, please talk to me ... Carol ... !"

Ann and I enjoyed a celebratory drink in the lounge.

Carol immediately filed for divorce, and two weeks later sent the photographs to Karen's husband at his office. I received a card from Carol several months later. She was doing well in her work, her parents were helping her care for the children, and she was looking forward to her new life, free of the dishonesty and suspicion she had lived with for so many years.

11

Woody

Sharon was livid when she received the videotape of Larry and Karen kissing in the parking lot of the Hyatt Regency at North Lake Tahoe. I was pleased with the success of this assignment, especially considering the difficulty factor. Casinos don't allow photographs for reasons of security and privacy. In fact, the fastest way to get your arm broken is to be caught taking photographs inside a casino.

Of course, that's where our two lovebirds were spending most of their time, so capturing them in a compromising position was pure luck. There they were—kissing and fondling in the parking lot. Camera, action, cut! That's a wrap. Sharon got her money's worth. Case closed.

Not exactly.

When Sharon saw the videotape, she just hung her head and cried. Then she uttered the words that have become so familiar to me over the years: "Why? How could he do this to me? What am I going to do now?" I suggested to Sharon that she get away by herself or go with a friend, go first class all the way; and above all, to be sure and put the entire expense on her husband's American Express card! But I could tell Sharon was seething inside, and I had an uneasy feeling that I was witnessing the calm before the storm. Although she didn't seem like the vindictive type, I was concerned.

Before I left, I offered a few words of wisdom. "Sharon, remember: the only person you will hurt is yourself if you do anything to get even. It may very well come back to haunt you. For instance, if you turn your husband in to the IRS, then it will be your half of the community assets they'll take. If you destroy his car, half of its value is yours. And remember this, above everything else—don't poison, stab or shoot your husband! He's not worth it." With that I left, trusting that I had her attention.

Two months later Sharon called me. She was about to leave on a vacation. "I'm packed and I'm taking the kids to Disney World. After that we're going on a three-week cruise."

"Good!" I replied. "Everything work out with Larry?"

"Kind of."

She was reluctant to give any details over the phone, so we arranged a lunch date at Scott's Seafood in Walnut Creek for the next day. I arrived early to visit with Bob Solario, a personal friend and the public relations manager for Scott's, along with Ford Andrews, the managing partner. I asked Bob for a table where I could talk freely without being overheard, and Bob asked the hostess to find me a table with a view of the reservation desk and off to the side for privacy.

I no sooner sat down than Sharon came in from the direction of the valet parking lot. She was wearing a flowery dress, which showed off her now slim, shapely, and tanned body. Varoom! She immediately came right over to my table, and I introduced her to Bob and Ford. They greeted Sharon and then offered us a bottle of wine or a choice of a dessert from their menu. We were both made to feel very special, and God only knows how much Sharon needed to feel special.

"Wow, Sharon, you look fantastic."

"Thank you, Greg; you're not just saying that?"

"Hardly. You've lost weight, firmed up and look years younger."

"You're making me blush."

"I think you're going to be doing a lot of blushing from now on."

"So you want to know what happened to Larry?"

"Fire away."

And she did; about how this wasn't the first time for Larry, and just how much nerve the son-of-a-bitch had. "I would never have believed he would do it again. And, with of all people, *the same married bitch as before!* Needless to say, you can imagine how extremely disappointed I was to hear their plans unfold on a recorder I purchased after the first go around. I decided to trust your experience and keep a monitoring device activated just in case he tried it again. You were right on. Larry and Linda were making plans for the second week of April. Asshole told me Tuesday evening that he was going to host a "guys only" fishing trip at our cabin at Donner Lake. Yea right! Bull. Larry's plan was to leave work on Friday, the fifteenth, and drive straight through to our Donner Lake cabin and prepare it for Linda who was driving up early Saturday morning. So when I heard about their scheme on Monday, the eleventh, I decided to really mess up their arrangements. I told Larry that I was going to visit my parents in San Diego the weekend of the fifteenth. I then placed a call to my doctor and told him I needed medication for insomnia; contacted the *Contra Costa Times,* and placed an order for a classified ad to appear Saturday and Sunday the sixteenth and seventeenth; and, last but not least, I contacted Diane and asked her if she could watch our daughter after school on Friday until Saturday afternoon.

"I spent the early afternoon shopping for the sexiest teddy, panties, bra, and garter. A pair of black high-heeled shoes and a seductive black dress completed the ensemble. Next I headed for Safeway and purchased steaks, potatoes, salad mix, and a very expensive bottle of red wine. By 3:20 p.m. I was leaving the Safeway parking lot and hoping to get on the road to Donner before the Bay Area traffic swallowed me up. I arrived at the cabin by 7:40. I tapped on the door, my arms full of grocery bags. The door swung open and Larry was facing me, his mouth wide open and a stupid grin on his face. The scumbag managed to stammer out, 'Uh, what are you doing here?' But I just played it off by reminding him how he always said he wanted me to be more 'spontaneous' in our relationship. That caught him off guard, and he said that I could only stay until the morning, when 'the guys' would be showing up. I agreed, but promised that this evening would be just for us so he'd really miss me."

"We lit a fire in the huge stone fireplace. I broiled some steaks while he ran off to the store to pick up some sour cream. I was sure he wanted to escape so he could call the bitch and make sure she didn't arrive until after I left. We enjoyed a candlelight dinner, music, and all the trimmings a romantic evening promised."

She paused to take a deep breath. I was about to ask her how she could find the fortitude to pull off such an Academy

Award-winning performance, when she interrupted my thoughts.

"After dinner I stood up and removed my black dress, and motioned to him to stand up and dance with me. While dancing to a very romantic slow song, I removed each and every bit of clothing Larry had on him. I took him in to the bedroom and sat him on the bed and said, 'Larry, honey, I don't want you to move a muscle.' With that I went to the kitchen and poured Larry and I two glasses of red wine. I went back to the bedroom where Larry was waiting patiently for my return, and gave a toast: 'Darling, I'm going to fuck you like you have never been fucked.' "

"We clinked glasses and drank our wine. Minutes later Larry was out like a light. By grabbing onto the bottom sheet, I was able to drag him off of the bed, pull him across the bedroom floor, through the door, and into the living room. In the center of the living room there's a large wooden beam from the ceiling to the floor. I spread his legs and rested his testicles on the beam."

"My next job was to go through the entire cabin removing any evidence of my visit. After finishing my final inspection of the cabin, I walked up to Larry, who was still peacefully passed out. I bent over his body and placed some surgical gloves on my hands, and I held his little penis up to the beam. I reached back into my purse and pulled out a syringe filled with Super Glue and applied it all over the underside of his penis and testicles. I pressed his little prick up to the hardwood beam, and then gave a quick tug on his ankles so his testicles were pressed firmly as well. Wow, it's amazing how fast that stuff hardens!"

"His little limp dick, all two inches of it, was firmly molded to the beam, and his testicles were flattened up against it as well. He looked so peaceful, he was even snoring! I thought this method was far less aggravating than confronting him and having it turn into an awful argument and him hitting me."

I was pondering the wisdom of her actions and the possible repercussions. Sharon continued with her tale of vengeance.

"I knew he'd wake up with the full realization of the hurt he'd brought my way and his horny little tramp would be the one to find him. They'd be spending their precious weekend figuring out how to separate the beam from his shriveled up little dick!"

My imagination was running at top speed now. I couldn't help but moan in sympathy for the poor schmuck, but the whole scenario also had me in tears of laughter. I was able to compose myself enough to ask, "So how did Larry separate himself from the beam?"

"Well, the rest was filled in by Larry. You see, Larry was so upset with me that when he came back down the mountain he wanted to have me arrested. So his statement to the police gave me all the details. Larry stated he awoke at 8:00 the following morning and found that he was stuck to the beam. By noon his slut arrived, found him Super-Glued to the beam, and called 911. Six young firemen arrived with ax in hand and stormed the front door only to find Larry lying in the middle of the floor glued to the beam. Well, the six young firefighters couldn't contain themselves and burst out laughing, which humiliated Larry big time. Then the firefighters called for an ambulance. Four firefighters placed Larry on a body board and raised him off the floor while the other fireman used a power saw and cut the beam just inches below Larry's balls at a 45-degree angle. Then they lowered Larry back down and used the same power saw to cut about six inches above

Larry's dick. Larry was very upset that the firefighters were taunting him. Larry's humiliation was tested again when the EMT's arrived, laughing and hooting louder than the firemen, and lifted Larry and the body board on to a gurney. Imagine Larry flat on his back with a sheet draped over the beam."

The crowd that gathered around the cabin laughed as they took Larry off to the nearby emergency room. Larry was even able to hear the description of his predicament on the mobile radio.

"Mobil Med to Tahoe, do you receive?"

"10-4, Mobil Med."

"We have a white male, late forties, penis SupeGlued to a wooden beam!"

"You have a what?"

"White male, late forties, penis Super-Glued to a wooden beam," he repeated.

Larry claimed that upon arrival, the emergency room doctor and staff were red eyed from laughing and trying desperately to look concerned and professional. The attending physician informed Larry that he could remove the beam in one of two ways. "We could surgically remove the skin attached to the beam and graft, if need be."

"Like hell! Get this fucking beam off me without cutting me!"

"We could also use acetone by injecting it between your penis and testicles and the beam, but it will probably take longer and burn like hell."

Sharon said Larry opted for the acetone. "Two hours later they successfully remove Larry's dick from the beam, along with his testicles, still intact. Larry was heavily sedated and sent back to his cabin with the slut, his penis and balls rolled up in gauze and tape."

"He spent the weekend alone. I guess his little bimbo had more exciting things to do than wait on his lordship and listen to his misery. She was also concerned that this time around her husband may have been informed about her relationship with Larry. Duh, you think?"

"It was several days before Larry could drive. He spent the time pondering what it would be like to come home. He knew I was beyond the realm of angry and hurt. And those extra days had given me time to empty the bank accounts, see an attorney, and begin arrangements for my future happiness, without Larry."

"Oh, in case, you're wondering why I took out newspaper ads: Saturday and Sunday garage sale. I sold just about everything Larry owned and loved, his golf clubs, suits, ties, boat, and turned in his rifles and guns over to the police. Just about everything I hated that he owned and loved, I sold. Gotcha!"

Sharon happily divorced, has found her self-esteem, and is dating a very nice man. Larry would do anything to have her back. No way "Woody"!

Oh! On a final note: Larry took his attorney's advice and didn't pursue litigation against Sharon for a very good reason. Larry didn't want his story showing up in public records. I won't tell if you don't.

12

Bashful Bob

Susan was a tall, trim brunette with an air of style and control. She was in her late forties and had been married twice before. Her first husband died in a boating accident. He had been young and successful, and left Susan financially secure with an infant daughter. Her second husband, older than Susan by ten years, was also a financial kingpin in his own right, but constantly had affairs behind her back. The marriage endured for six years and produced a son.

When we met Susan, she had been married to husband number three, Bob, for ten years. He was in his mid-thirties, didn't have a dime to his name, worked as an administrator at a nearby medical facility, and was well educated. At the time they married, Susan felt he had possibilities, but over the years she has seen a repeat performance of her second marriage—infidelity strikes again!

Susan was not the typical client Ann and I usually meet. For a change, this was not the financially dependent wife hoping for a fair settlement from the evil philanderer. Instead, Susan had all the marbles, and she had been very careful not to invest them in any community property. She also had in her possession that wonderful legal masterpiece of the twentieth century, a signed and sealed prenuptial agreement.

For quite some time, Susan had been investigating Bob's activities on her own. She had caught him with another woman five years ago, a receptionist at work. He was warned to cease and desist immediately or be fired. But Susan was seeing red flags again, and now she said he had really gone over his head.

"I can't be 100% sure, but I think ... and again, I'm not positive ... but I think he's traded in the receptionist for the boss' wife, Celeste."

Ann and I nodded to each other. We'd heard this scenario before; and if Susan were correct, this would be an easy assignment. After receiving our retainer, we followed up on Susan's suspicion by putting Celeste under surveillance. Celeste was a socialite and rarely idle. She arose at sunrise and attended meetings, luncheons, and more meetings until late into the evening. Each time Celeste entered a building, we weren't sure if she was attending a meeting or meeting Bob. Because of her gender, Ann put the most time into this surveillance. She was able to walk through the meeting halls, gather informational brochures, and leave without raising an eyebrow—something a man would not be able to get away with in a room full of women.

One afternoon, around two o'clock and after four different meetings in the East Bay, Celeste made a surprise visit to the Lafayette BART station to board a San Francisco-bound train. I dropped Ann off at the station and she also boarded the train. She kept in communication with me by cell phone while I drove my car across the Bay Bridge to San Francisco. Celeste got off the train at the Union Square Station while Ann followed and kept me informed as to where they were going.

Celeste headed straight for Sak's Fifth Avenue and bought some lingerie. Next stop was the cosmetics counter for toiletries and perfume. Then she went into the corner pharmacy and purchased a toothbrush, toothpaste, and a small tote bag. Much to Ann's surprise, she said she also saw Celeste drop a tube of lipstick into her pocket. This woman had the money to buy out the entire store but felt compelled to steal a small tube of lipstick! Ann was confident today was the day Celeste was meeting someone interesting, and she was willing to bet a month's expense account that it wasn't going to be her husband!

Celeste left the drug store and Ann followed. Meanwhile, I parked the car and, thanks to being able to stay in communication with Ann, was able to catch up with them as they entered a four-star hotel. Since Ann had been around Celeste in Saks and at the drug store, I knew it was time to give her a break before our prey "heated up." I walked past Celeste and Ann and then in a boisterous voice, I called out to Ann, "Hi Honey! I need to pick up something in the room. I'll meet you in the coffee shop." On that cue, Ann veered off towards the coffee shop.

I was waiting at the elevators when Celeste arrived. As the elevator door opened, I turned towards her and asked if she was going up. She stepped inside and asked me to hit the button for the 14th floor. "Me too," I said. I pushed the button for the 14th floor, held the door for her when we arrived, and proceeded to follow her down the hall. She stopped at Room 1420 and gently knocked on the door. I walked by reaching for my "pretend" key.

As the door opened, I overheard a man's voice asking, "What kept you?" She went inside and closed the door. I waited a few minutes, then tiptoed back to the room and listened to the dialogue inside. I heard a lusty male voice passionately exclaiming, "Oh Baby you look so good!" The only response was our socialite's distinctive giggle, heavy breathing, and a whimper. In record time, they were hot and heavy in lust. But I couldn't prove anything until I found out who checked into Room 1420.

I went down to the coffee shop to confer with Ann, who was enjoying a Danish with her coffee. "Well, our hunch to follow Celeste today paid off. She's in Room 1420. I heard a lot of heavy breathing and some cries of 'oh-Baby, oh-Baby.'" But now came the important part. We had to prove the unidentified man was our Bob. Easy. As long as there are security guards who want to become private eyes, we have an almost infallible source of information.

I went down to the garage of the hotel. A nice young man named Steve was the manager of security for this area. I asked him if he could assist me on a very sensitive case. "Steve, (not his real name) this is highly confidential. Can I trust you to keep it under your hat?" Steve nodded, his eyes shining as he stepped closer to hear me whisper.

"Steve, I'm a private investigator and I need to know who is registered in room 1420. Can you help me?"

"What's going on?" Steve replied.

"We believe a very high-profile female is paying a visit to a very high-profile male in the room, and they're not married to one another. I represent one of the spouses. This is so very confidential that I will never tell them where or how I got the information, OK?"

With that, we shook hands and I left the garage. In my pocket was the printout of the hotel bill and the proof I needed. Bob's name was plastered all over it, along with his credit card number and his signature. All we had to do now was to try and catch him leaving the hotel. I set up surveillance across the street while Ann waited inside near the elevators for a chance to videotape him. We couldn't be sure he would leave the hotel via the main elevators; years of experience have taught us that service elevators and stairways are always an option for someone who likes to keep the intrigue going after the show. Nevertheless, we knew we could put him and Celeste in Room 1420, which is what our client wanted to know. We lucked out because Bob and Celeste left the hotel by way of the main elevator right into the grand lobby. Just as the elevator doors opened, Ann, armed with her video camera and telephoto lens, was able to capture Bob's final kiss on Celeste's cheek and his love pat on her elegant bottom—all with date and time!

Ann then contacted Susan to tell her what had happened during the day. Susan was absolutely delighted to hear we had a copy of Bob's signature on the registration form, plus videotape displaying the scene, date, and time of Celeste's waltz into the hotel. Gotcha!

Susan paid us handsomely for our efforts. Like most of our clients, this woman was totally fed up with men (I couldn't blame her in the least). Being that I was a member of the enemy camp, I merely received a "Thank you, nice job, Greg." But she took a particular liking to Ann, and even offered her a job.

Many months went by. Then one day we received an invitation to a formal charitable affair that Susan was hosting at her home. It was a good cause and we were happy to attend. We were especially pleased when Susan enhanced our reputation by hailing us as the best private investigators she had ever hired. (Of course, we were the only ones she had ever hired!) We had a wonderful evening and rubbed elbows with the rich and famous—all potential clients. We also had a chance to hear Susan's story about how she evened the score with her former husband:

Susan lived in a stately home in Piedmont, a community situated in the Oakland hills overlooking the San Francisco Bay. When Bob was living there, his calls to Susan were not toll calls because his office was nearby. This made it difficult for Susan to check the phone bills for clues when she first suspected Bob's wandering eye. But what she really wanted was to be able to monitor any phone calls and record the numbers dialed. She had mentioned this to us when we first met and I told her I would look in to it.

The week after Ann and I captured Celeste and Bob at the hotel in San Francisco, I received a call from one of my sources. He told me about a recording device that would get the job done, and then some. Susan purchased one of the units and that's the last we heard about it until the night of the party.

After finishing dinner, Susan invited us to join her in the study. She closed the door, asked us to sit down, and then told us how she had used the recording device. She explained how her husband never called Celeste at home, but he did get messages over his Message Manager. Using the unit, she had been able to record, decode, and display Bob's access number and his four-digit password. This allowed her to access his messages at any time, day or night, without his knowledge. She smiled as she told us Celeste would leave messages with the day, time, and place for each rendezvous.

The last message Celeste left for Bob was just before Christmas. "Stan is visiting his northwest offices in Seattle and Vancouver and promised me he would be home no later than midnight Christmas Eve. How about you coming over at eight and keeping me warm? I'll have a cozy fireplace and lots of pillows. You can give me an early birthday present."

Susan, filled with the spirit of the holidays and revenge, found out that Celeste's birthday was the day after Christmas. She thought how nice it would be to arrange an impromptu surprise party! She immediately began making arrangements by contacting Stan's secretary and asking if she would mind helping to organize a surprise party for her boss's wife. The secretary was delighted, and jumped in with both feet. The most important detail that Susan had to work out was to get good ol' Stan back to the Bay Area in time for the surprise. This was accomplished when Stan was told about the surprise party and he agreed, in the spirit of celebrating his wife's birthday, to cut his skiing holiday short.

Susan had one other card to play. She had to figure out how to keep the party guests out of the house until after Celeste and Bob had begun doing their thing, and decided the poolside cabana would be the perfect place for the guests to gather. It was out of view of the main house and had its own driveway, so they could all sneak into the house through the garage.

Her plan was really starting to look good! All she needed to do now was to have Stan tell Celeste he would be calling her from Tahoe at 8:30 p.m. on Christmas Eve, but he would really be calling from his own backyard! If Celeste answered, they would know she was home and everyone could sneak in.

"D-day" arrived, and Susan and Stan met for a drink at a restaurant near the Oakland Airport at 5 o'clock on Christmas Eve. Susan didn't want anyone to see Stan and then let Celeste know he was in town. Stan's secretary took care of making sure the guests parked at various locations along the exclusive boulevard, and then quietly ushered them up the driveway and into the cabana. They were all waiting quietly in the cabana, gifts in hand, enjoying drinks and *hors d'oeuvres*, when Susan drove up the driveway with Stan. At precisely 8:30 she asked him to call the house.

There was no answer! Just as Susan was about to panic big time, they heard a splash. "She's in the pool," Stan whispered. "This will really surprise her!" On command, the entourage of 27 guests joined their host as he walked out of the cabana's side door and down the path to the pool. They were halfway through their chorus of "Happy Birthday" when they reached the edge of the pool. The pool lights reflected Celeste and her dear friend, Bob, in their birthday suits. Both of them were huffing and puffing, splashing, and slapping the water into a frenzy of waves, leaving no doubt as to what they were up to at the shallow end of the pool. Celeste was the first to see her guests and started furiously pounding on lover boy's shoulders to stop.

The silence was deafening as the partygoers froze in a state of shock. Then they all started shuffling back towards the cabana. It was clear no one wanted to share in Susan and Stan's humiliation. Stan appeared pale in the glow of the pool lights. Susan was barely able to hide her delighted grin. There wasn't a sound, and the only movement was the steam rising from the warm water that was now eerily calm. Bob and

Celeste cowered on the stairway in the shallow end of the pool, hugging their knees, in an attempt to cover their nakedness. For them, there was no place to go. Susan could hear Bob's usual, uncultured commentary whenever he didn't know what else to say. "Shit! Shit! Oh Shit!"

Celeste just stammered as she desperately tried to fabricate a convincing story for Stan. It was useless. Stan looked at Susan and said, "I guess the surprise was on you and me. Care for a drink?"

Susan divorced Bob and, under the circumstances, he quit his job. He tried to find another job in the same industry but nothing seemed to be available. He's convinced he was blackballed. (Do you think?)

Stan also divorced Celeste and, as life would have it with the very well-to-do, she received a healthy settlement. Susan said her only regret from the whole incident was that Stan had been an innocent victim of her hoax.

Unfortunately, Stan was the big loser in this case. He was not only broken hearted by the events on Christmas Eve but was humiliated in front of his employees and friends. He had to pay his wife a large sum of money to boot. We tend to forget the broken hearted spouse of the other party because we very rarely see them. I have learned that most men and women want to know if their spouse is being faithful or not. Do you tell? The answer is a resounding ... yes!

13

░▚░▚░▚░▚░▚░▚░▚░▚░▚░▚░▚░▚░▚░▚░▚

24-Hour Spa

The list of rendezvous sites is only limited by the imagination.

There are the back seat quickies that remind them of their high school days. And of course there's the "Mile-High Club" and the yacht to Catalina, just for some variety. But for those of us who don't fly or sail, there's a new den of solitude called the neighborhood spa. Springing up in your local strip mall, these cesspools of seduction are the ultimate in something different to offer the loving couple. Each hot tub is surrounded in privacy, and the management usually has strict rules about divulging just who their patrons are. They're usually open for the better part of 24 hours. Each room comes with a spa, towels, and robes, all for less than the price of a motel room. Instead of a television, there's a prophylactic dispenser. And when you get a little too steamy, there's a chaise lounge where you can finish the rest of your wine.

Linda was married to Greg for 11 years, and she made it a point to let me know that they didn't have children. She had always wanted children, but Greg was too immature to have them. Coupled with the fact that he was sterile, children just didn't seem to be in the cards for them.

Greg was having a difficult time dealing with the sterility factor, and it wasn't long before Linda suspected that he was having an affair. She called me to confirm her suspicions, and in an attempt to learn what he was planning to do about their marriage and assets. I asked Linda if she had an idea of whom he was seeing, and she told me that she thought it might be a woman who lived in San Francisco. Linda had tried to follow them on her own, but she couldn't get anything concrete. She would follow them from one shopping center to another, but all they seemed to do was talk … period! Obviously exasperated, she finished by blurting, "I can't figure them out!"

I explained what was happening. Lovers need companionship, sex, and lots of communications to feel good about what they are doing. They rehash their feelings day after day, hour after hour, constantly reassuring each other that what they are about to do is the best plan. He says "I love you and I want to be with you forever." She says, "When are you going to tell Linda about us?" He replies, "Any time now."

Translated this means:

He said, "I really love banging you."

And she's saying, "When are you going to dump the bitch and make an honest woman of me?"

"Any time now" is guy code for "not in this lifetime, stupid."

Get the picture Linda?

"Well what does he see in her?"

"The same thing all men see in the other women: 'sex with a twist.' Something different!"

"So you don't think he will leave me?"

"I don't think he'll leave you for her. But I also think that if you beg him to stay with you, you won't be doing yourself and your psyche any good. We'll catch him on video kissing and fondling her in public, and then you can decide what to do about it."

Friday night was a good night to follow Greg. He would be driving Linda's newer Buick, and there would be children's toys left in the car from Linda's child care business. There was always an assortment of stuffed animals, buckets, and clothing left from their day at the park. Tony, one of my "agents," had a plan to place a "bug" in a child's stuffed toy. The night of the surveillance I met with Tony, who produced a stuffed gray mouse with a long tail. The bug was sewn into the mouse's nose and the tail concealed the antenna. Our mouse was placed on the center console of the car, where Linda kept miscellaneous change, hairpins, etc.

The moment Greg came home he started an argument with Linda. This helped him feel justified in storming out and driving away. As Linda had predicted, he drove off in her Buick. Tony and I tailed him from Pleasanton to the BART Station in Walnut Creek were he meet Terri, a shapely brunette in her late twenties. In comparison, Linda was a good five years older and 30 pounds heavier.

After stopping for gas at the local Exxon, Greg proceeded to Taco Bell on Main Street. He parked his car in the back and they entered the Taco Bell. I parked my surveillance van next to Greg's Buick, got in the back, and turned on the receiver while Tony waited in position across the street. The recorder was rolling, and we were ready to gather the information Linda needed to assess Greg's plans. Greg and Terri were back in their car within 20 minutes, and started talking about their plans as soon as they started the Buick's engine. Greg told Terri that he desperately wanted to have children, but couldn't because Linda was barren. The car didn't move, and after five minutes, Greg turned off the engine and just continued their discussion, which was just a rehash of how desperately they needed to be together, how Linda didn't have a clue about his needs as a man, and that he just needed a little more time to put his affairs in order before leaving her for good.

Another hour passed and they finally turned the engine of the Buick back on. They drove through Walnut Creek and Concord as though they were lost. Finally, they drove up Contra Costa Boulevard and into a shopping center parking lot, where they proceeded to enter a 24-hour spa. Tony and I parked our vehicles, one on each side of the Buick with room for a few cars in between. Tony, who had Linda's spare key, opened the door to the Buick and quickly grabbed the mouse, and then entered the spa. Greg and Terri were still at the front desk making arrangements to rent a room and spa for an hour. I plugged my receiver into my video camera and recorded both the audio and the video of them making their arrangements. Approximately one hour later, Terri and Greg were returning to their car. Tony was right behind them, mouse in hand, picking up their conversation. Greg walked around to the driver side and Tony walked behind Terri. When she arrived at the passenger's side Tony offered, "Let me get that door for you Miss." And as Tony began to close the door, he bent over and exclaimed, "I think this dropped out," and handed the mouse back to her. Terri thanked Tony and she and Greg continued their love talk for another hour, talking sweet nothings about how great they were together and how much they should be together forever.

Linda received the video and audiotape the following day. She agreed with me that she felt Greg was just using Terri for sex, and that Terri was expecting the payoff to be marriage. Linda decided that Greg was too immature for her and that she was far better off getting on with her life. But she didn't rush into a divorce. She began to squirrel her childcare money away. She bought new clothes and began to take better care of herself. She joined a health club and gave herself a much needed attitude adjustment before taking the big step.

Greg and Terri never did marry. In fact, Greg broke off his relationship with Terri as soon as he was served with the divorce papers. Greg is still trying to win Linda back; and the last I heard, her answer is a resounding, "NO!"

14

The Mile-High
Club

On a warm August evening I received a call from a very
formal lady, educated and classy, with excellent communication skills. After she ascertained that I specialized in
domestic cases, we arranged a meeting at the Brass Door
restaurant in San Ramon the next day.

Esther, having just entered her early sixties, had maintained a very petite, curvaceous figure. Her thick, once dark
hair was now nearly completely gray. For quite some time
she had suspected her plastic surgeon husband of having an
affair, and was at her wit's end trying to find out where and
when the trysts were taking place, and with whom.

Jules, her husband, was also in his sixties, sporting thinning salt and pepper hair, a short, rounded physique, along
with a prominent nose and accent rooted in his New York
childhood. As a successful plastic surgeon, Jules had
acquired many of the toys a man of wealth enjoys: a shiny

and very expensive Mercedes Benz, the grand home in an exclusive community, a private airplane, and quite probably, according to his wife's suspicions, at least one girlfriend. When Esther dared to share her concerns with Jules, he gave her the brush-off and told her to take up a hobby. And that's just what Esther did! She took up the study of investigations and made me her instructor.

During our meeting the following day, Esther provided me with photographs of her husband and details about his two offices, daily habits, their automobiles, and the Beechcraft Bonanza airplane he kept in a hanger at the local Buchanan Field Airport in Concord. Esther made it a point to tell me that Jules had two offices, one in San Francisco and the other one in Palm Springs. And this is why he had the plane, so he could fly from one office to the other. He was the best "boob man" in the business, according to Esther, who proudly sported a pair of her husband's silicone assets. (My mind wandered to visualizing the grandmothers of the future. Instead of rosy-cheeked, round and cuddly, they might be suctioned, perked up and glamorized once a year by their neighborhood plastic surgeon.)

The following Friday afternoon, Ann and I placed Jules' San Francisco office under surveillance. It was 5:30 p.m. when we saw him leave the second floor elevator and head towards his silver Mercedes convertible. Even though August nights in the San Francisco Bay Area are usually warm, this doesn't necessarily hold true in "The City." In the early evening the fog begins to roll in; but despite the slight chill in the air, Jules removed the top from his car and drove to the restaurant at One Market Street with his salt and pepper hair blowing in the breeze. Upon arrival, the valet took his car and parked it along the street just off Market, and Jules entered the restaurant.

I dropped Ann off at the front door of the restaurant. She was appropriately dressed for a casual evening in San Francisco. She wore moderate heels, a flirty summer dress, and her long dark hair flowing down her back. I left my car and a $20 bill with the valet, who assured me that my car would be parked in front of the restaurant for a quick get-away. I showed the valet my credentials and told him I was on an assignment, adding a little zing and romance to the occasion … sooo Hollywood!

I entered the restaurant in search of Ann. There she was; sitting right next to our subject! Good work! This place was difficult to get into without a reservation, and even Doc Jules must have had a reservation. I sat down across from Ann and whispered, "How did you manage this?" Ann smile proudly and confided that she had tipped the maitre d' $20. Our profit margin was being eaten up in tips!

Ann and I each ordered a glass of wine and a dinner salad. We paid the bill, including coffee and tip, so we could get up and go at a moment's notice. Jules sat alone, quietly sipping his wine and nibbling on some of San Francisco' famous sourdough French bread. A few moments later, Ann and I were struck by a stunning Asian woman who approached Jules' table. She spoke in a near whisper, which made it impossible for Ann and me to eavesdrop on their conversation. She was the epitome of the exotic Asian beauty, with dark almond shaped eyes, creamy olive complexion, a small turned up nose, rosebud lips, and waist-length shiny black hair. Ann and I strained to overhear their conversation.

"Lilly," he said, "It's time that I take you flying with me again. Let's fly up to Fort Bragg and spend the day together?"

"I'd like that," she giggled.

They agreed to meet the following morning at the airfield in Concord.

Other than casual conversation about how they were going to spend the following day at Ft. Bragg, and polite talk about the health of Lilly's parents, there was no real indication that Jules was carrying on an affair with Lilly. We followed Jules and Lilly to her home in San Francisco's Marina district. Jules drove Lilly up to the curb of her home. She quickly gave him a kiss on the cheek, opened the car door, and rushed into her apartment building. Of course, I had a video of this good-bye, which didn't add up to anything resembling a possible affair. Jules drove a few blocks, pulled over to put the roof back on his car, and then we followed him back to Contra Costa County to his Diablo home.

Since it wasn't too late in the evening when Ann and I arrived home, I called a local pilot, a fellow member of my athletic club. I called but got his message machine (this guy is single, an ex-fighter pilot, and the night was still young). I left a message for Bob to call me, no matter how late. At 1:20 a.m., Bob's call woke me.

"Bob, can you manage a flight tomorrow morning?"

"Sure! What's the gig?" he asked.

"There's a Beechcraft at Buchanan and I need to follow it to Fort Bragg."

"No problem! What's going on?"

"This is very confidential, Bob. I need to follow a suspect and his friend who are planning to spend the day there."

Bob said he would file a flight plan and meet me at the airport at ten o'clock.

Ann and I woke at eight to a clear summer morning, enjoyed our customary caffeine jolt and made a quick perusal of the local newspaper. Afterwards, I pulled out my camera bag and began to organize the video and SLR camera equipment, keeping in mind the options for weather conditions and lighting. The tripod and binoculars were packed too.

Ann and I dressed in layers. Although it promised to be a dry, hot summer day in Walnut Creek, Fort Bragg is located to the north, on the coast, and is usually quite cool. Russian fur traders originally settled this seacoast town, but its modern allure is the quaint village atmosphere of nearby Mendocino, fresh sea air, panoramic vistas of the rugged coast, and rich history. Why were Jules and Lilly on their way to Fort Bragg? We presumed it was for a day of sightseeing and romance.

This would not be a relaxing day for Ann or me. The only time we can take a break is when our subjects are enjoying a sit-down meal. You can let your guard down in a restaurant because you know nothing too touchy-feely can happen. After dinner is usually when things get interesting.

Ann and I arrived at Buchanan Airport and met Bob promptly at ten o'clock, leaving us time to kill before Jules' arrival. Bob found out where Jules' Beechcraft was located, filed his flight plan, and performed his preflight checks. We were ready and just waiting for Jules and Lilly's arrival.

Ann spotted Jules' Mercedes pulling into the parking lot, where he took a few minutes to talk with two men. We kept an eye on him as he wandered back towards the parking lot where Lilly was just pulling up in her car. Jules greeted her with a wave, walked briskly up to her car, and opened the driver's side door. There were no public displays of a kiss, hug, or any physical contact other than Jules offering his hand to assist Lilly out of her car.

Jules and Lilly headed towards their hanger, and we headed over to our hanger to board Bob's plane. I asked Bob how he was going to be able to follow Jules and Lilly, and he said that he would wait until five minutes after the Beechcraft's departure, and assured me that he would be able to catch up to them quickly. True to his word, we followed Jules' plane from afar, finally flying past them and landing at the small private airfield near Fort Bragg. We waited for their arrival from our rental car, which, of course, was ready and waiting. Jules and Lilly rented a Lincoln Town car, and we followed them into town.

Ann and I had anticipated that Jules and Lilly would spend the day sightseeing and shopping, followed by dinner and a stay in a local Bed & Breakfast. At least that's what we would have enjoyed if we had the day to ourselves. They spent the afternoon wandering through shops, and enjoyed a late lunch at an outdoor café. Occasionally, they would share a quick embrace or hold hands. Of course, Ann and I had the cameras ready to capture what Ann likes to refer to as "Fuji Moments." But we didn't have anything on film that you could sink your teeth into. It was all fairly tame and could easily be dismissed by a smooth-tongued philanderer.

Unexpectedly, at 4:30 we were en route back to the airport and soon thereafter following Jules and Lilly back to Concord. While Jules and Lilly were in their hanger tying down their "bird," Bob excused us from this job so that Ann and I could be waiting for our subjects in our car. Would Jules and Lilly go to a local hotel for their tryst? Why here and not in romantic and secluded Fort Bragg?

Ann had the video camera rolling, and I had the SLR clicking away to capture what we hoped might be a telltale pat on the bottom, a territorial embrace and kiss at the car. Lilly and Jules emerged from the hangar and walked across the parking lot towards Lilly's car. Lilly's hair was untidy and Jules appeared uncharacteristically disheveled. What happened?

Bob approached us and noticed what had caught our undivided attention. "Looks like a member of the Mile-High Club," he said. We had read J's *Everything You Ever Wanted to Know About Sex But Were Afraid to Ask,* but didn't think it possible. Maybe in an airplane with a fully manned cockpit and an in-flight movie, but not in a private plane with only the two of them and no one else to pilot. But Bob shot back with a confident, "Sure they could!" He then proceeded to give us our first lesson in the finer points of aviation as he explained about the Beechcraft's autopilot. Bob added, "A warning signal will go off if another plane is coming too close."

I think the whole idea is pretty impressive and the ultimate in daring. It would explain a lot too. But I still don't know how anyone would be able to concentrate on sex at 8,500 feet!

Ann and I had to regroup and come up with some ideas to catch Jules the next time he tried this daredevil lovemaking feat. I called Esther and asked her how often Jules traveled to his Palm Springs office.

"Once or twice a week."

"Would you know in advance of a pending flight?"

"He's really good about letting me know when he'll be away."

I was thinking that we might be able to plant a listening device in his plane. It would monitor all the sounds in the passenger cabin. I told Esther about my plan and she replied, "It's too bad that you can't somehow videotape them."

"Hold on a second." I thought for a moment and realized that I might just be able to do that with a "pinhole" video lens mounted on a miniature camera with a transmitter or videotape recorder. I told her as much, and asked if she would be able to make the plane available for us to do the wiring.

"No problem there," Esther assured me. "I go out to the airport with Jules every couple of months or so. The fellas out there know me well enough. I don't think they'd think anything of my being out there or you being with me."

We decided to go with a time-lapse videotape system that was activated by a motion detector. Our power source would be leeched from the plane's circuitry. The moment anyone entered the cabin, the camera would begin filming and would automatically shut off after a few minutes when there was no motion. I contacted an electronics supplier and had everything professionally installed the following week. It was two weeks after the installation of our video equipment when we heard from Esther that Jules would be flying to Palm Springs late the following morning.

I just love it when everything works! When Jules returned from Palm Springs, Esther accompanied the electrician and me to the airport so that we could retrieve the video from the plane's cabin. As Bob had suspected, the video confirmed that Jules had, indeed, joined the Mile-High Club. I'm surprised he didn't have a heart attack! He was in such a hurry, there was no time for gentlemanly courtesy. Lilly did not appear to be any too comfortable as Jules mauled her. Her skirt was raised, her panties were pulled down, and he was finished before she had a chance to say, "Where's the airsick bag?" Though it was apparent Lilly was not pleased by the experience, you could tell by her resigned expression that she was used to it.

Our job was done and Esther's was just beginning. She would be analyzing her thirty plus years of marriage and deciding what she was going to do. Knowing your husband is having an affair because you saw a photograph of him going into a motel room with a woman is certainly enough to poison any marriage to the point of divorce. But sometimes a picture is truly worth more than words can say, and this was one of those times. How could Esther ever put the images on this video out of her mind?

Still, thirty-five years of marriage is a lot to give up on. Maybe, with some financial leverage, she could save her marriage and feel fairly sure that Jules would never cheat on her again. Jules would have to sign over his interest in their multi-million dollar home. She would also insist that he give her a large sum of money in her own account. In return, she would give him another chance to win back her trust. He understood that if she caught him cheating again, she would immediately file for divorce, and the remainder of their assets, past, present and future, would be split 50/50.

Esther was wise to first check on the status of their community assets. Was Jules hiding any assets? Esther had all the marbles accounted for before she approached him with the evidence and his choices.

Several months later I contacted Esther to see where she stood with Jules. Jules had broken down in tears when he saw the tape, and pleaded with her not to leave him. As Esther's ultimatum dictated, Jules instructed his attorney to prepare the documentation necessary to transfer all ownership in the home solely to Esther. A very generous lump sum was also deposited in a separate account for Esther. They continued to live together as man and wife; and with the help of marriage counseling, their marriage is on solid ground and they are enjoying their early retirement years. Knowing Esther, I think Jules is now an inactive member of the Mile-High Club.

15

Snowbound

It was mid December. The day was overcast and a light snow was falling. Ann and I arrived at Squaw Valley by noon, registered at the lodge, and were given the key to a room that overlooked the gondolas that carry skiers to the slopes. We were not sure if Stan and June would attempt to ski; ski season was late that year, and there were areas of exposed dirt and rocks on the slopes. Our first objective after getting settled was to locate June. A week prior to our arrival, our client had learned through a telephone bug that this was the woman her husband, Stan, was meeting for a ski weekend at the corporate condo here at the Squaw Valley Lodge.

At our first meeting, Stacy could be described as a plump housewife with lines on her face that revealed premature aging, most likely from stress. Stacy had been married to Stan for 18 years, and certain signs had led her to believe he might be seeing someone, so she set up a voice-activated recorder on the phone. When she contacted us a couple of days later, she said she wasn't prepared for what she had heard on the recorded phone conversation.

Stan was making plans with someone named June to go skiing over the weekend. He told her that his "little domestic goddess would be so busy with baking and doing what she does best ... cleaning ... that she probably wouldn't even notice I'm gone."

Ann and I knew when a husband talks about his future ex-wife; he very rarely says anything positive. But Stan's comments about his wife would prove to be a big mistake.

We discussed with Stacy how we would catch her husband in the act. Knowing he would deny everything unless he was caught red-handed, our job was to videotape him and his little snow bunny in any compromising positions we could. We cautioned her not to let Stan know she was aware of his plans.

"You mean I have to pack the bastard's bags?"

"Sure. Send him on his way with your blessings. You might even want to pack a treat or a love letter for him. Just don't do anything to alert him!"

Stacy somewhat reluctantly agreed and said she would continue to play the role of dutiful and loving wife. Early that evening, Stan arrived home from work to the smell of fresh-ly baked bread. He attempted to snare one of the slices but was caught in the act. "No!" Stacy said, "Not until dinner."

After dinner Stacy, Stan, and their youngest daughter each carried a plate of freshly baked dessert, along with some hot tea, to the family room and made themselves cozy. Later, Stan complimented Stacy for being such a wonderful cook and homemaker.

As we had suggested, Stacy packed Stan's bags and tucked in a love note:

"My dearest, please drive safely, I love you so ... Stacy, XOXOXO."

Ann and I walked around the lodge and soon caught our first glimpse of June, who was a real looker. She was dressed in red ski pants and a white angora sweater, standing about 5'4" with red hair, and she reminded me of a young Jane Fonda. It was easy to see why Stan was attracted to her. Ann and I decided to eat dinner and retire early, because we knew the following day's events would require all of our stamina. We had already purchased our lift tickets so we wouldn't need to stand in any lines. We could just stick close to June and Stan.

At six o'clock the next morning the sky was still dark. We slipped out of bed and enjoyed a quick cup of coffee in our room. I went outside in the predawn chill to see if I could spot Stan's silver 300E Mercedes in the parking lot. After a brief tour of the area, I didn't see it and thought, "Good, maybe we can enjoy a hearty breakfast."

By 7:15, Ann and I were seated at a window table that overlooked the front of the lodge, with a premium view of all the cars coming and going. Just before eight o'clock, we saw Stan drive into the parking lot. Ann and I had already paid our bill and were relaxing over a cup of coffee, waiting for the games to begin.

Before Stan came in the front door, Ann left our table and strolled towards Room 440, which we had identified as the one where June was staying. From a distance, Ann watched Stan as he got out of the elevator. He was carrying a bag and went straight to the room and knocked. June opened the door. I caught up with Ann and we waited.

When the couple emerged from the lodge, June was dressed in the same outfit as the day before, except she had added white gloves, a white furry hat, and a pink parka. Stan was wearing long white ski pants, a blue parka, color-coordinated gloves, and a knit cap. Stan's thin legs were accentuated by the white stretch pants and bulging parka. I nicknamed him "Chicken Legs." Streaks of gray hair around his temples escaped from the edging of the knit cap.

Looking at Stan, I couldn't help but wonder what it is that women see in some men. What was appealing about June was obvious. She was 10 years younger than Stacy, and obviously provided more than a little excitement. Stacy herself, though perhaps having let herself go, still catered to her husband's needs and provided him with beautiful children and a cozy home. But what was it about Stan that was so appealing? What the hell did Chicken Legs provide to either of them?

Ann and I boarded the tram that would take us to the slopes. We knew the trip would take about 10 minutes, and then we would have to wait in line at the gondola that would take us up the mountain. After we got off the tram, we maneuvered our way through the crowd so we would be seated behind Stan and June on the gondola. We're always careful to never make eye contact with a subject if we can help it. We may have to be close to them for two or three days, so it's important they don't see us observing them.

Fortunately, we were the first four of six people to board, giving us an opportunity to sit at the back while Stan and June sat up front. During the entire ride June and Stan were holding hands, kissing, whispering sweet nothings, and giggling. As they exited the gondola, Stan patted June on the rear. I had hoped we would be able to get some film footage of the lovebirds smooching, but no such luck.

On my way down the mountain, I rounded a steep corner and spotted Ann standing behind some trees with her little camera out. I came up to her and saw the subject of her picture. There in a clearing was Stan and June, attempting to help each other up from a major spill. Stan must have landed in a thin patch of snow because there was dirt embedded in his white stretch pants. From the mascara under June's eyes, it appeared she was crying. She planted a pole for Stan to grab while he attempted to stand up. Ann and I thought they might have been injured, but in a few moments, they were skiing down the slope as aggressively as ever. They left us in the shadows as they sped down the hill.

Since I was the keeper of the video camera and couldn't risk a major tumble, Ann was better able to ski more swiftly and, within a few minutes, she caught up with the duo. This time it looked as though they had landed in a mud puddle. The back of June's ski pants was soaked through and Stan's pants were now more of a brown color. As they quickly recovered and skied down the hill, I was able to videotape them. But then, to our surprise, instead of getting back in line for another ride up the mountain, June and Stan went to the tram area for a ride back to the lodge!

We caught up to them at the boarding area and were immediately educated as to the need for their hasty departure from the slopes. The stench coming from the two of them was reminiscent of an outhouse. June was crying and Stan was red-faced. No wonder ... because they were drenched in shit! The intestinal noises we heard were followed by a steady flow of foul smelling liquid.

The tram driver immediately ushered them to their personal seats at the back of the tram, while the rest of us waited for the next tram. Meanwhile, I was videotaping everything from a distance and Ann was capturing it all "in living color." Needless to say, the lovebirds didn't have the time or the presence of mind to notice Ann and I recording their hasty departure back to their room.

That evening, Ann and I were surprised to see Stan and June at the bar. We positioned ourselves so we could overhear most of their conversation. They were trying to piece together what they may have eaten that morning to cause their malady. Could it have been the cocoa they had before hitting the slopes? Then June suggested the brownies were the culprit, but Stan assured her that it couldn't have been the brownies because the family had them for dessert the evening before. "Besides, I had to search the refrigerator to find them. Stacy didn't leave them out for me." Stan stood by his Stacy's brownies. In fact, he planned to finish the remaining two that evening.

The couple spent the remaining hour talking about their relationship, with June pushing Stan to make the ultimate decision to divorce Stacy as soon as possible. "As soon as possible" was Stan's loophole. He gave June all the pat answers as to why they had to wait and begged her to be patient just a little longer.

We knew Stan had no intention of marrying June or divorcing Stacy. He had the best of both worlds; a wonderful wife and mother for his children, along with a willing sex partner on the side who had nothing better to do than dote on his every whim. We also knew that Stacy held the cards now, and you could bet money that June would never become the next "Mrs. Chicken Legs."

Heavy snow began to fall as the sun disappeared behind the mountain. Ann and I were cozy in the lounge but suddenly sprang to attention when Stan and June were leaving. We tailed them towards the parking lot and followed them by car down the road to Truckee. We hoped they weren't going to be heading for the Tahoe casinos, or this would be a long night. Thankfully, they stopped at a Mexican restaurant on the main street of downtown Truckee. We followed them inside and saw that the dining area was large and had many intimate nooks for dining. We were seated one booth away from the loving couple, and while we feasted on chips and salsa, Stan and June enjoyed enchiladas, rice, and refried beans.

Suddenly, Stan jumped out of his seat! His face was flushed and perspiration glistened from his brow and upper lip. He had a look of panic as he sprinted towards the men's room. I casually got up from my seat and followed. As I approached the door, a young man was leaving and whispered, "I don't think you want to go in there, pal."

His advice was unnecessary. The stench and the noises reminded me of a traveling companion who often bragged he could eat anything ... and then downed a burrito from a vendor at a park in Mexico City. Need I say more?

As I was returning to our table, June jumped up and ran towards the ladies' room. I immediately noticed June's eyes as she passed me, and was reminded of deer caught in headlights. I observed bulges in her pantyhose accompanied by the sound of gurgling and farting. This was not a pretty sight, especially in a restaurant. Moments later, patron's and employees began evacuating the restaurant, Ann and I included. The stench overtook the entire place. The sounds of dueling farting from both bathrooms drowned out the mariachi music. Ann and I went directly to our vehicle and moved across the street so we could have a good photo opportunity to catch the party poopers' exit. Within a few minutes, most of the guests had left, and a few employees dared to re-enter the restaurant. We videotaped Stan and June coming out the front door, yelling at each other—June in bare feet, no pantyhose, and Stan with a large dark area showing on the rear of his slacks.

When we finally returned home, we shared the photos and film footage with Stacy, and she shared her brownie recipe with us. Her revenge was truly sweet.

Stacy ended up divorcing Stan. And because he was no longer "unattainable," his appeal to June lost most of its luster. Now he was just another divorced man paying support and living on leftovers. June had bigger fish to fry!

Stacy's self-confidence grew, and she discovered there were many men who truly appreciated someone like her. It didn't take long for her to find a new partner to share her life.

Stacy's Get 'Em on the Run Chocolate Brownies

- *One package brownie mix with chocolate syrup and nuts. Follow printed instructions.*

- *Frost with your favorite chocolate fudge frosting recipe, adding melted chocolated laxative (think "Ex-Lax"), confectioner's sugar and milk "to taste."*

- *And remember ... don't lick the bowl!*

16

The Rodent

We've all heard of the "small-man complex." In my experiences, I've found this complex and infidelity have a tendency to walk hand-in-hand. This is a funny story about a small man, but he's not laughing.

Frank, 5'7" and 130 lbs., was a successful insurance defense lawyer for a large Seattle law firm. He had always had the gift of gab and could charm the birds from the trees, which came in very handy in his line of work. Outside the courtroom, his areas of expertise were baseball, dancing ... and women.

His marriage to Kathy was in its 14th year, and they had two children. Kathy had worked while Frank went to law school, supporting him through those difficult years both emotionally and financially. After he graduated, they got married.

By the time their oldest child, Davy, was 12 years old; he could look his dad eye-to-eye. Their 10-year-old second son, Sean, seemed to be following in his brother's footsteps in the height department. (There must have been a recessive gene from their mother's side of the family.) Like many attorneys, Frank would frequently call to say he wouldn't be home for dinner because he had to get ready for the next day's hearing, or he had to meet with a client. Kathy was used to this and wasn't particularly concerned, until she began to notice the not-so-subtle changes in his personal hygiene and wardrobe. He began wearing very expensive suits and spending more and more time tending to his personal appearance. She often caught him looking at his reflection, making sure every hair was in place. New personal hygiene products appeared in the bathroom. Kathy hadn't seen Frank fuss over his appearance that much since the early days of their dating. But now, Kathy was not the one being courted.

"What do you think about this?" Kathy asked me.

"Has there been a noticeable weight loss?"

"No," Kathy replied. "He's always been thin."

"Have you received any late night hang-up telephone calls?"

"Now that you mention it, yes, I have."

"How about the car?"

Kathy looked at me like I was a mind reader. "We just got a new sports car."

"What kind?"

"A new Porsche."

"To answer your previous question, I'd say there's a good chance Frank is seeing another woman."

Kathy didn't want to hear this and at the same time she did. "That bastard! What can I do? I'm not a lawyer. I can't fight him. His friends and the judges he knows will gang up on me.

I'll lose everything ... including my children." I couldn't help but wonder if Frank had planted this scenario in Kathy's head over the years.

Kathy said she had confronted Frank with her suspicions and had threatened to divorce him. Of course he denied an affair, and threatened her with total devastation if she even thought of getting a divorce. "Relax, Kathy," I assured her. "He's just trying to scare you. Remember, he has a lot to lose. When do you think Frank first began 'stepping out'?"

"When the little prick started spending too much time fiddling with his hair."

I asked her to give me a call the next time Frank got all dolled up, and we would figure out just what he was up to. The following Thursday morning, Kathy called.

"Hi Greg. This is Kathy, the 'rodent's' wife. I spoke to you last week."

"Sure, Kathy ... I remember. Is today the day?"

"I think so. He spent an inordinate amount of time in the bathroom this morning, singing and lathering up. He put that shit on his hair again and nearly waltzed out of the house. It was everything he could do not to jump for joy."

Kathy asked me to "pick him up" at work and stay with him all day and into the night if necessary. Ann and I made preparations for a long day of surveillance and packed our video camera, one 35mm SLR, and sound equipment. We arrived at Frank's law firm at 9:45 that morning and immediately found his brand new Porsche in a parking place with his name on it. We took up separate positions to make sure we'd catch Frank, no matter what, and chatted and joked via our radio hook up to pass the time. We were armed with all the pertinent information Kathy had given me during our first meeting. We had a recent photograph and a list of people, places and interests. We also had all of Frank's telephone numbers, including his cellular number.

We didn't have to wait too long in the dark garage. Frank entered the garage from the building's side exit and walked towards his car. "Don't you think this is an unusual time for Frank to be leaving for court?" Ann whispered over the radio.

"Affirmative. Let's roll."

Frank made a beeline for the SeaTac Hotel and parked in the rear parking lot. I radioed Ann to park her car right in front and not worry about a ticket. "I'll follow him to the back, and then come up front later to re-park your car while we trade places so you can learn where he's going."

I watched Frank get out of his Porsche and pull a small overnight bag from the trunk. I followed him from the rear parking lot into the SeaTac, weaving my way through the corridors of the first floor and out into the main lobby, where Ann was patiently waiting to take over. I traded car keys with her and went right out the front door to where her car was parked. I moved it to the parking lot in the rear so we could follow Frank later if we needed to.

I went back into the SeaTac and attempted to locate Ann on the two-way, but got no answer. This usually means it's time to be quiet because she may be standing next to him and can't talk. After another 10 minutes went by, Ann finally signaled me on the radio

"Hi Honey! Where are you?"

"In the lobby." I answered.

"I'll be right there!"

A few minutes later, a smiling Annie stepped out of the elevator. "He's on the seventh floor in Room 730 and he didn't have a key."

"You mean someone was already in the room?"

"Wow, you're quick," she teased. "He just knocked on the door and in a moment, the door opened. I could hear a woman's voice, but I couldn't stop to look without drawing suspicion."

"Now we just have to sit around and wait for them to come out. Were you able to get any video of him entering the room?"

"No, but I did get a video of him walking down the hall towards the room."

"That's good," I said.

Ann and I got a cup of coffee and resumed surveillance at two different locations in the hotel. Ann was in the back towards the rear parking area and I was in the main lobby watching the elevators. At 2:30 p.m. Ann radioed that the loving couple had just come out of the stairway door and were heading towards the parking lot. I jumped up and headed immediately towards the rear of the hotel. Ann was already in her car. I had just enough time to get into mine before they drove out of sight.

"Ann, where are you?"

"I'm right behind them."

"As I left the parking lot, I drove right past Frank's Porsche. What are they driving?"

"They're in a maroon Cadillac with a white top."

I could see it in the distance and raced towards the traffic light. There was Ann, directly behind them. Apparently, the couple was heading out of town. Since I knew they had never drawn a bead on me, I traded places with Ann and we tailed them to a quiet seafood restaurant. Frank walked around to the passenger side and opened the door for his companion. *Tres gallant!* I wondered, when was the last time he showed his wife the same courtesy? It's too bad these philandering men don't take the time to romance their wives any more.

They might regain some of those tender feelings that have been lost over the years.

The couple was seated in a quiet booth. Ann and I sat at the bar in an adjoining room where we could keep an eye on them, and even get some video. As we were observing them, we noticed Frank scratching his head. His lady friend scratched her head also. Was it the power of suggestion?

Moments later, their lunch arrived. An employee walked past with a carpet sweeper, the manager directly behind him. They both seemed intrigued by their work. Frank was surprised that the restaurant employee seemed to be trailing them from the entrance to their table.

Suddenly Frank complained in a loud voice, "What the hell is this in my salad?!" The manager approached the table and looked at the salad, but Frank soon answered his own question.

"Oh my God. It's hair!"

With a look of disgust, he pushed the plate towards the manager. In the next fraction of a second, there was a scream from Frank's date. "My hair! It's my hair!" she screamed frantically and jumped up. Up to this point, we hadn't seen anything out of the ordinary; but when she stood up we could see a large clump of long hair in her fist and a noticeable dent in the back of her hairdo. For about 10 seconds, Frank was silent. His mouth was moving, but no words were coming out. Then loud enough for everyone to hear, he yelled, "Damn! My fucking hair is falling out!"

They both ran from the restaurant and we followed. We weren't too concerned they would see us, because I don't think they would have noticed a parade following them at this point. They were frantic. They headed straight for a medical center. We waited nearly two hours for them, and when they finally returned to the car, we videotaped them with their bandaged heads.

We contacted Kathy and gave her the video. We could tell she was savoring her moment of revenge as she sipped a glass of wine and watched the tape. She hadn't told us of her plans, of course, but now she gave us the juicy details of how she patiently, carefully got her ducks in a row, gave Frank just enough rope to hang himself, and got the larger part of the community assets as the result of proving Frank's infidelity and breach of trust. She laughed wickedly as she told us Frank wanted to sue the manufacturer of the shampoo he used, everyone and anyone! She added that she doubted he would stand a chance of winning because the "Nair in the Hair Shampoo Revenge" was her way of letting him know he'd been had!

Kathy continued, and we learned this was only the beginning! She had also sequestered as many of the liquid assets as she could, filed for divorce, and watched Frank's 5'7" stature in the community shrink. Not only did Frank not have any hair, but he also ended up not having a job. His bald girlfriend was the wife of his law partner!

17

⬚⬚⬚⬚⬚⬚⬚⬚⬚⬚⬚⬚⬚⬚⬚⬚⬚⬚⬚

Gullible No More!

Karen, whose face and body had seen better days, lived in one of those beautiful Tudor homes in an exclusive Hollywood neighborhood. She had everything in life that a woman of 40 could want—a handsome husband, a vacation home in Aspen, her own Mercedes, and her only child in a reputable college. But her marriage was miserable and collapsing rapidly. She had always feared this might happen, but it was how it happened that crushed her.

Jeff, her husband, was always gone. Even when he was home, he was gone. Although he was four years her senior, Karen suspected her looks out-aged him, and that he had started looking elsewhere. In fact, she was so certain of this she sometimes wished he would tell her the truth and let her off the hook. But she knew that was just not in the books.

Karen was desperate to talk to someone who cared. She didn't want to tell her family, friends, or neighbors about her marital problems, but she badly needed to confide in some-one. One day after a blow-up with Jeff, Karen thought, "It's time to do something about this mess."

Just then, the phone rang. She picked it up and heard a familiar voice. "Hi Kay! What about doing some serious shop-ping?" It was Jen, one of Karen's best friends. They had known each other since elementary school days when every-one used to call Karen by her nickname, Kay. Like Karen, Jen had everything she could ever want. She lived with a dynamo from the film industry in a beachfront home in Malibu, had a fancy car, and owned vacation homes in Aspen and Maui.

Karen smiled as she thought to herself, "The two things that take my mind off of Jeff are having sex and shopping." She immediately agreed to meet Jen for an early lunch. They would park their cars at the restaurant and go from there to the shops.

Karen decided to enjoy a steamy bath before meeting Jen. The earlier fight with Jeff had been draining. Besides, a woman needed to be in the right frame of mind to go "charg-ing" around Beverly Hills. Finally it was time to get dressed. She put on slacks, a baggy blouse, loafers, and threw a sweater over her shoulders. Of course, she grabbed her cred-it cards.

When Karen arrived at the restaurant for lunch, she noticed Jen's car was already parked in front. Jen was a year older that Karen, but she had taken advantage of all the plas-tic surgery money could buy. She always said it wasn't because she was vain—it was only to please her husband. In any case, she had an incredible figure and didn't look a day over 27. She was often stopped on the street because people thought she looked like a young Ann Margaret and wanted her autograph.

Karen slipped into her chair and greeted Jen. "As always, you look incredible. I suppose I should seriously consider having a few tucks myself." They laughed and got down to the serious business of planning their attack on the posh stores in Beverly Hills.

"Where do you want to start off?" Karen asked.

"Only one place ... Rodeo Drive!"

Once they had laid out their agenda for the day, they turned to the menu. Both decided on a salad with avocado and shrimp. When the waiter left with their orders, Karen took a deep breath and then said, "Jen, I need your help!"

"Of course! What's going on?"

"I'm becoming suspicious of Jeff. He won't communicate with me at all. He just seems more and more into himself. I know he has a high profile job, but this is different. We don't mess around like we used to. No teasing each other ... no family get-togethers ... I'm beginning to think there may be another woman."

"Oh no, Pumpkin!" Jen exclaimed. "I just wouldn't believe that from Jeff! He adores you!"

"I'd like very much to believe it's just my imagination, but there are so many little clues. He called me last week and told me he was finishing a project at the office, so he'd be a few hours late coming home. I thanked him for letting me know, because we had made plans to meet with some friends that evening. About ten minutes later, I remembered something I needed to tell him, so I called right back. His secretary said he wasn't working that day. I thought that seemed rather bizarre, but didn't dwell on it. Later, when he finally got home, I told him he had missed a nice get-together at his favorite restaurant and asked how work had gone. He said he was sorry he'd had to miss out, but he had been under pressure to finish a job at the office. He lied to me, Jen."

Karen looked around the room as though trying to pull her thoughts together, and then she continued. "Recently, he told me he was going on a fishing trip out of Long Beach over the weekend. He said he just wanted to get away from the pressure and go where there were no phones, no faxes, just total freedom from all of today's electronic leashes. He said he'd be at sea the entire weekend. I asked him what charter service he was taking, and he said the usual one, Skip's Fishing Charters. He told me I wouldn't be able to reach him, even if it was an emergency, but assured me he would be home Sunday night. He left on Friday, dressed in casual clothes and armed with his deep-sea fishing pole and gear. After he pulled out of the driveway, I called Skip's Fishing Charters and asked if Jeff was confirmed for a charter. The man I talked to said they were booked for the next three weeks, and the name Jeff R. was not on any of their lists. So I started calling all the fishing charter companies, and every one of them told me the same thing. No Jeff R. I had been lied to again. But that's not all. Besides the lying and the late nights, he's spending more time on his personal hygiene and has bought some new clothes, shoes, and other things." Karen looked Jen straight in the eye. "I'd say I have a cheating husband."

"Oh no, Hon! Jeff loves you," Jen assured her. "He may just be having a bad month or two and has a lot of pressure. Give it some time."

"I'd like to think you're right." Karen sighed. Then she brightened. "Anyway, thanks! What are friends for but to perk each other up now and then? Come on! Let's eat and get out of here so we can do some serious therapy." They both laughed. While they ate, they reminisced about friends they knew in school, the boys they dated, and the fun they had. They paid their tab and headed for the stores.

Midway through their shopping frenzy, they stopped at a fashionable shop that offered lattés to their customers. They sat at one of the tiny tables for two and sipped their frothy chocolate coffees, waiting for the caffeine jolt to take hold. Feeling comfortable again, Jen turned to Karen.

"Tell me what happened after the fishing trip."

"Oh the 'shit' came home with a fish alright!"

"So he went fishing after all," Jen noted.

"No, I don't really think so. Especially since there was parsley stuck to the underside of the dorsal fin, a la Safeway! When I asked if I could go with him the next time, he told me they didn't have facilities to accommodate women—just guys. He also assured me I wouldn't like it. He's such a liar!"

Karen's relationship with Jeff continued to get worse after the shopping spree. Pretty soon he started giving her generic answers that she couldn't check up on. She figured he probably realized she was getting suspicious. All during this time Jen was a real friend. She was there to listen and offer a shoulder to cry on.

After a while, Karen decided she couldn't stand not knowing any longer, so she hired Ann and me. I could tell she took an immediate liking to Ann. I think it's because Ann doesn't look like a private eye. She looks more like a soft-spoken schoolteacher.

We talked about Karen's suspicions and agreed it was very likely her husband was seeing another woman. Naturally, Karen wanted proof. She handed us an envelope marked "CONFIDENTIAL." We told her we wouldn't have too many clients if we blabbed things all over town. "Your information is safe with us," we assured her. Inside, neatly typed, was some background information on her husband.

Karen then proceeded to tell us what we had heard before from far too many other women. She talked about the late nights, Jeff not being where he said he would be, his improved personal hygiene, her finding a lipstick under his car seat, their frequent arguments, and the constant lies. We could tell Karen was truly miserable and frustrated, and she wanted her misery to come to an end as soon as possible.

She then told us about Jen and how she was so thankful she had this one friend she could confide in. We cautioned Karen that from now on, she was not to divulge anything to anyone—not even Jen. Karen said she had already told Jen she was going to hire an investigator, so we asked her to let Jen think she was still looking for someone and explained why we had to be so strict about this.

"It's the old saying, 'loose lips sink ships,' mixed in with Murphy's Law," I told her. "We have to do everything possible to be sure that our cover isn't blown."

Karen agreed and asked how long it would take. "Maybe a week or two at the most," I told her. "This is assuming he is having an affair and he's in town for the next few weeks."

"Well," Karen replied, "I can practically assure you he's seeing someone. As far as I know, he's planning to be local for the next few weeks."

Ann looked over the three pages of information Karen had provided about Jeff. It revealed where he worked, his gym, his favorite golf course, good friend's homes, office telephone number, cellular number, private home line, favorite restaurants, and ex- girlfriends' names, as well as a list of possible current girlfriends. There was also a current photograph of Jeff, a description of his cars, and a listing of his hobbies and interests. Karen had even included a calendar of dates and times Jeff could be expected to be at the golf course, gym, or at work. It was an impressive summary. After reviewing the information, Ann asked Karen a few more questions.

"Does Jeff own his own business?"

"Yes," replied Karen.

"Do you have authority to enter his office?"

"I guess I could go there. I've been to his office many times, but never without him being with me."

"Karen, does Jeff bring the bills home to pay? We're especially interested in the office phone and cellular phone bills."

"No, he doesn't. All of the bills are paid at the office."

"Do you have keys to his office?"

"I might. There are so many keys around the house. I don't know which keys go to which locks though."

"Does Jeff have a private entrance?"

"Yes. He has one on the third floor of the parking garage."

"So he can come and go without anyone knowing he's gone."

"Sure," Karen replied. "But he wouldn't do that! He's very conscientious about having his employees know where he can be reached. Jeff is a stickler for being able to respond promptly to a customer's calls and requests. He's very good that way."

I told Karen we would begin our surveillance and investigation the next morning. In the meantime, I arranged for one of our agents to sweep the house for bugs and telephone taps.

"What for?" Karen asked.

"Just in case Jeff has your phone bugged to see what you may be doing. I wouldn't leave any messages on your home phone recorder or talk to you on an unsecured line. We'll get together as necessary for a cup of coffee or whatever. But you'll know it's me and we can make arrangements to meet, okay?" Karen agreed and Ann and I left.

Early the next morning, we parked near Karen's home to begin our surveillance. At 6:30 a.m., our eager beaver pulled out of the garage in his Lexus 400 and headed towards Santa Monica Blvd. He drove east towards town, got off on Wilshire, and pulled into the garage at his office complex. He parked on the third level, where he entered his office through a private entry, just as Karen had told us. I found an ideal parking place where I could see him if he left his office, and Ann went downstairs and placed herself so she could watch the main entry to the building.

We were both outfitted with earplugs and small portable radios, and after a few minutes, Ann radioed me that there was a styling salon next to the office building. I immediately came up with what I thought was a brilliant idea and offered her a trade. If she would bring me a bag of donuts and a cup of coffee, then she could spend the morning at the salon being pampered. I figured, how long could a manicure take? Chances were that our bird wouldn't be flying during the morning hours anyway. Besides, if I saw any movement, I could easily contact her.

Ann agreed that my idea was brilliant, and she didn't even say anything about my diet. The donuts and coffee arrived in record time; and after we enjoyed our little breakfast, Ann went to the salon. The location of the manicurist's table gave her a clear view of the lobby and front door. Her earphone was discreetly tucked into her right ear under masses of waist-length brown hair.

Waiting for something to happen was boring beyond belief. I decided to pass the time by whispering sweet obscenities into my sweetie's earphone. I knew it was a nasty thing to do to a woman who has to sit still while having nail polish applied, but it was fun nevertheless. Little did I know what she had in store for me! At her first opportunity, she got up and went to the ladies' room, radioed me, and told me off in no uncertain terms! My ears burned for an hour. I promised to behave.

Then my little Annie sweetly asked if she had time for a pedicure too. What could I say? Anyway, it was only 10 o'clock—lots of time before the mass exodus for lunch.

So there I was, sitting in my car picking donut crumbs from my sweater while my wife was sitting in the beauty parlor having her feet massaged. What's wrong with this picture? At least I was in her good graces again ... I hoped.

Nearly an hour had passed when the private entry door opened and there was Jeff! I quickly radioed Ann that our bird was getting ready to fly. I had positioned myself so I could see both Jeff and the salon, but it was difficult keeping my eyes on Jeff. The salon door flew open and out ran Ann, barefoot, with little swabs of white tissue between her pink toes, her shoes in one hand, purse in the other, heading straight towards my car. Nothing like drawing attention, Annie! But it was just a false alarm. All our boy did was remove something from the trunk of his car.

By then, Ann was sitting next to me, paper stuck between her toes, three of which were polished and all of them dirty from running on the sidewalk without any shoes. After a brief, but effective, lecture on crying wolf and embarrassing her to the point of hysterics, Ann returned to the salon to finish the pedicure. Walking into the salon on her heels, swabs between her toes, she received more than a few stares. I could just imagine the story she had to come up with to tell the pedicurist. What a trooper!

I sighed. This was not turning out to be a good day.

Ann finished at the salon, had the parking ticket validated, and returned to the car. As she handed the ticket to me, she gave me a kiss and mumbled something about adding the false alarm to our long list of things to laugh about one day. I promised not to get her going with anymore "I thinks," and that next time our quarry would have to get in his car before I sounded an alarm.

Noon came and went. Finally, at one o'clock, Jeff left the office, got in his car and headed towards Beverly Hills. We followed him to the Beverly Hills Hotel where he parked his car and walked towards the lobby. With the videotape camera cleverly hidden in her fashionable handbag, Ann trailed him into the lobby area. I came through a side entrance. We saw Jeff sitting on a couch. Ten minutes passed and we heard his name paged. He went to the phone, but all Ann could hear from the one-sided conversation was, "No problem. I'll wait." A few minutes later, we were a bit surprised to see two men in business suits enter the lobby, shake hands with Jeff, and go to the dining room for lunch. We had been expecting to see his date.

Ann and I decided to take the opportunity to have lunch as well. We ordered shrimp salads and paid the bill right away so we would not be stalled when we needed to go. Jeff spent two hours at the Beverly Hills Hotel, and then returned to his office. During the drive back, Ann set up the scanner to monitor Jeff's cellular calls. She programmed his number into the online computer and then waited for him to call someone interesting. We heard him check his voice mail at 3:15. It was a woman's voice saying, "Call me." Jeff punched in a speed dial number and a sultry voice answered the phone, "Hello."

"Hi ya' Honey. I got your message. When did you call?"

"At two. Where were you?"

"I was at lunch with a future big account. It lasted longer than I thought, but it went well."

"When are we going to get together again?"

"I need to be careful. We should only get together when I leave town. Tell you what; I'll take you with me to Vegas in a few weeks. That will give us a lot of time together."

"I'm not going to wait a few weeks to fuck you!"

"Well, neither am I. I just want you to be patient with me while I figure out the when and where. I have way too much money to lose."

"You've been socking it away, haven't you?"

"A certain amount of it I have, but I keep dipping into it to advance my business efforts. I'm on the brink of really breaking out from a good business to a great business. This would not be a good time to face a bunch of fucking lawyers in a divorce suit. Ummmm, I want your beautiful hard, nude body all excited for me, Baby!"

"I don't want to wait either. Let's try for tomorrow afternoon. Okay, Honey?"

"Alright."

"What time should I call you?" The mystery woman asked.

"Leave a message on my voice mail and I'll call you from the car where it's safer."

"Okay. Until tomorrow. Love you!"

Ann immediately called Karen and asked her to meet for a cup of coffee. She was already sitting at a corner table when Ann arrived at the Starbuck's. It was apparent she was very nervous. As gently as she could, Ann told Karen that Jeff was definitely having an affair. "We don't know the name, but we do know they're planning to meet tomorrow."

Karen was visibly shaken. Ann tried to reassure her that what we were doing was for the best and, in all likelihood, we would have an answer for her tomorrow. Karen looked as if she was going to burst into tears at any second, but since it's easier to keep your emotions in check in public, she was able to hang on to her dignity.

Her voice quivered as she asked, "You don't know who she is?"

"No. We just have her voice on tape. He didn't call her by name. He just referred to her as 'Baby.'"

"That's what Jeff called me when we were dating. Where do we go from here?"

Ann replied, "There's a good chance Jeff will be meeting her tomorrow. She's going to call him on the cellular phone and, hopefully, that will give us a clue about where they're going to meet. As soon as we know, I'll call you and say 'star' and then hang up. We'll meet you here. Now, are you going to be all right?"

Wiping a tear from her eye, Karen said, "I can manage."

"It's important that you don't say anything to Jeff tonight when he comes home."

"Oh, I won't! I have far too much invested in this ordeal to blow it now."

"Good," Ann said, "I'll call you tomorrow."

I had waited outside in the car while Ann talked to Karen. When she got in, I asked, "How did it go, Babe?"

"Don't call me that!"

"Are we being a little overly sensitive?"

"Can it, Clouthier! Karen's heart has just been ripped out. I hate this part of the job."

The following morning, Ann and I drove both of our cars to Jeff's office building. We parked in the garage—my car on the third floor and Ann's on the first floor—and took turns watching the front of his office. No matter which one of us was on foot, we knew we'd be able to quickly get to our car and be ready to follow Jeff at a moment's notice.

It was 11:20 when Jeff left his office. Ann was sitting in my car while I was watching the front entrance. She radioed me to get ready because Jeff was heading out. I hurried to Ann's car and hopped in, waiting for Jeff to arrive on the first floor. Ann gave me a blow-by-blow account of his every move.

I pulled in behind him as he came down the ramp. He drove out onto Wilshire Boulevard and towards the freeway. Ann was right behind me. Then he entered the on-ramp to get to Highway 10 towards Santa Monica. While we were driving, Ann let me know that Jeff was getting a cellular phone call. A few minutes later, as we whipped in and out of traffic after him, Ann reported the call was from our mystery lady. Again, her name wasn't mentioned.

"What did she say, Ann?"

"It's not what she said that's bothering me, it's what he said!"

"Okay, you have my undivided attention."

"He said he'll see her within two hours and told her he was on the way to the airport."

"Oh shit!" I said. "What airport?"

"I don't know!"

"What airline?"

"I don't know that either."

"Okay, if he heads south on the 405, then it must be LAX. One of us needs to beat him there. We've got to take a crap-shoot, Ann, and head for Southwest. They have the most flights going out. Damn! He's two hours away from her, which could mean San Francisco, San Diego, Vegas ... he could be going anywhere. Ann, you stay on him and I'll get to Southwest Airlines and hope he checks in with them before boarding."

I passed Jeff like a bullet. Ann stayed back and kept a mild pace behind him. Thirty-five minutes later, she tailed him as he drove up Century Boulevard towards the airport. Now if we were just right about the airline.

I parked my car and started running towards the Southwest Airlines entry. Ann called me on our walkie-talkie to get my position. When I told her, between gasps, that I was just two doors away from Southwest, she shouted, "Stop! He's entered the Alaska Airlines terminal and is heading for the loading dock."

"Oh hell! I have no idea where Alaska Airlines is from here. See if you can find out where he's heading. I'll try to catch up to him."

Ann tried to get through the security gate, but set off every alarm in the place. She wasn't armed, but she was wired from head to toe. After surrendering her walkie-talkie, she began a mad chase to the Alaska Airlines departure section and found Jeff in line for a flight going to San Diego. She tried to buy a ticket on the same flight but was told she would have to purchase one at the main ticket desk.

So much for a trip to San Diego. The way our luck was going, his lady friend would pick him up at the airport and they'd drive off before Ann could get some film on her anyway. Ann walked back to the security counter and picked up her walkie-talkie. I was sitting in a chair waiting for her.

"Did you find out where he was going?"

With a disappointing sigh, "Yes, he's off to San Diego."

"It can't be helped. We did the best we can."

"I know," Ann said, "but I just hate to see Karen under so much stress day after day. I thought we would be done today. I practically promised her we'd be able to give her the whole story."

"There's one thing we can't do in our business, and that's make promises," I reminded her. "Too many things can happen to throw off our best laid plans."

Ann called Karen and gave her the code word. We drove back to Los Angeles and directly to Starbucks. We were there only a few minutes when Karen arrived, anxiety etched over her tired face. Her first words were "Who is she?"

"We lost him at the airport," Ann explained. "He left LA via USAir on a flight to San Diego. He had his ticket in his pocket and we couldn't follow him."

"Oh, I see." Her face dropped towards her lap.

I reached across the table and took her hand. "Karen, I told you this case could take up to two weeks to finish, and it's only been a couple of days. I know you're anxious, but these things take time. However, we do have an idea of something that might work. Do you have a friend or relative that lives out of the area?"

"Yes, I have a sister in Boston."

"We don't mean anyone that you need to fly any great distance to visit. We were thinking of someplace you could go that's only an hour or two away by plane." Karen then told us that she and Jeff had a place in Aspen, Colorado, and could go there for as long as necessary. Ann helped her concoct a story for Karen to tell Jeff; that she'd be getting away for two or three days. That way, he'd feel safe enough to meet his girl and stay local.

"Okay. I need to get away from all of this anyway. I think I'll ask Jen if she wants to come with me."

"That's fine," Ann said, "but don't tell her anything."

"I already told her I called off hiring you. I think she'd enjoy coming to Aspen with me."

"Let us know as soon as you can when you'll be leaving."

"I'll try to arrange to leave the day after tomorrow, on Friday. I know Jeff likes his Fridays. Jen and I can leave in the morning."

Early Friday morning we placed Jeff under surveillance again. I parked where I could see the house, and Ann waited in her car at the intersection to the main street. I saw Karen drive out of the driveway on her way to pick up Jen. Jeff was still home, although Karen assured us he would be expected at the office. We waited until 10:00 a.m., and began to wonder if he had called in sick. Ann tried to call the home number on her cell phone, and Jeff answered on the fourth ring.

"May I speak to Kay?"

"I'm sorry. She's on vacation in Aspen. Would you like to leave a message?"

"That's alright. Will she be home next week?"

"Yes. She should be back by Wednesday."

"I'll call back. Thanks."

Ann relayed the conversation to me and then added, "I wish we had their phone wired! It would be nice to know ahead of time what he's planning." Just as I was about to agree with her wishful thinking, the garage door came up and I could see Jeff preparing to get into his car. I radioed Ann, and we were on our way.

From the way he was dressed—shorts, Hawaiian print shirt, tennis shoes, and sunglasses—it was obvious he wasn't going to the office. After a short drive, we ended up at Reuben's in Marina Del Rey. We saw Jeff greet a willowy, red-headed beauty and videotaped them having lunch. Then we followed them to the Marina Del Rey Towers, a secured community of high-rise apartments.

We showed our credentials at the gate and drove up the circular driveway, right past the loving couple. We could see they were headed for the elevators. I dropped Ann off. She knew what to do and arrived at the elevators just before the happy couple, putting her in control of the elevator buttons.

"Which floor?" Ann politely asked.

"Four," Jeff answered.

Ann hit three for herself and four for Jeff. When the doors opened at the third floor, Ann quickly walked to the stairway next to the elevator so she could get up to the fourth floor before the elevator. She radioed me where she was heading. She quickly pulled out her camera, hoping to get a shot of them exiting the elevator and walking to their apartment.

By now I was huffing and puffing my way up the stairs. When I finally arrived, breathless, at the fourth floor, Ann teased me, "Out of shape are we?" Then she added, "I have some footage of them walking to their apartment. Its number 415."

"Now all we need to do is find out who she is," I gasped.

We knew it would be a few hours before we would have to worry about the lovebirds flying the coop, so we went downstairs for a cool drink and some appetizers. The rest of the afternoon was an exercise in boredom. We watched his car, as well as the restaurant parking lot in case his lady friend had parked there. Having her license plate number would probably be all we would need to identify her.

Finally, at 7:30 in the evening, the couple returned to Jeff's car. We followed them to a seaside restaurant. They sat in a cozy, out-of-the-way table for two. Ann and I asked to be seated in the opposite corner where we could see them, but they wouldn't notice us. We enjoyed dinner and returned to the parking lot to wait for Jeff to leave. At almost 9:30 Jeff and his lover returned to his car and headed back towards Marina Del Rey.

"Oh, not this again!" Ann complained.

Jeff pulled into Reuben's parking lot and escorted the lovely lady to her Mercedes Benz that was parked nearby. I was hoping Jeff was no different than most men and was ready for the photo opportunity. Sure enough, as they reached her Mercedes Benz, Jeff put his arm around her waist. Click, click. He lowered his hand towards her bottom, patted it, and gave her a kiss as she put one hand gently to his cheek. Click, click. Ann made note of the license plate, which I made sure would be included in several of the photos. Then to be absolutely sure, we followed the young lady home.

The next morning we called Karen at Aspen. We told her that although we didn't have a positive ID on the other woman, we had what we needed to get the ball rolling and would certainly know who she was by Monday morning. We planned to meet at Starbucks at two o'clock Monday afternoon.

After hanging up, Annie said, "Let's pick up our photographs tomorrow ... early ... just in case we need reprints or enlargements, okay?"

"Something's bugging you. What is it?" I asked.

"I don't know what it is. I can't quite put my finger on it. I think it may have something to do with a comment Karen made when we first met." She chewed her lip as she tried to remember, then proclaimed, "Oh well, this case will be finished up for good on Monday, so let's just enjoy the rest of the weekend."

Monday arrived and we awoke to another day of Southern California's best sunshine and humidity. As we were eating breakfast, Ann's eyebrows formed into a scowl.

"You're still bothered by something, aren't you?"

Ann looked at me intently. "Remember Karen telling us that her best friend drove the same kind of car she does?"

"What are you thinking, Ann? It couldn't have been her because she's been with Karen. Besides, this is LA and nearly everyone drives a Mercedes or Beamer."

Ann persisted. "If you could describe Jeff's girlfriend, which motion picture star would you say she looks most like?"

"That's easy," I answered. "Ann Margaret!"

For a moment there was total silence between us.

"Well, let's just keep an open mind until after our meeting with Karen this afternoon, okay? Let's see what name comes back when we run the license plate on the mystery woman."

The afternoon arrived too quickly to suit Ann. The results were in and we waited at Starbucks for Karen. When she walked through the door, she seemed surprisingly at ease. There was a confidence and strength in her we hadn't seen before. Was this a magnificent effort to keep control of her emotions? No, Karen assured us. She had just enjoyed her time away. She'd done a lot of serious thinking and was feeling better about her options. "I spoke to a counselor in Aspen. She assured me that things usually work out for the best and the sooner I confront the problems, the faster the healing process can begin."

Ann was about to hand over the pictures to Karen when Jen walked in. Karen introduced us by name, "Jen, this is Ann and Greg." We all said our hellos and I stood to offer Jen a seat in our booth. As Jen slipped into the booth, Karen went on to say, "Jen, these are the private investigators I told you about."

"Oh?" As Jen replied, her face turned pale. She looked like she wanted to stand, but was trapped by Karen and Ann on one side and me on the other. She looked at Karen, "Uhh ... Kay, honey, why don't we get together another time when you're not so busy?"

Karen pleaded, "Jen, now is when I need you. Greg and Ann have the information I've been waiting for and I'm counting on you for moral support. I really need you here."

Ann also spoke up, "No, Jen, I think you should stay." And with that, Ann handed a brown envelope to Karen. "These are pictures of the other woman and her address."

Jen's shoulder's started shaking her eye's welled up with tears and began to weep. "Oh Kay, I'm so sorry. Please forgive me."

Karen's eyes grew wide and her mouth fell open. Without opening the envelope, she immediately knew whose photograph was inside. She took a deep breath and stood up in front of the booth. Without saying a word or even giving Jen a glance, she asked if we would give her a ride home.

Ann and I followed Karen to the parking lot, leaving Jennifer to deal with her guilt. I drove Karen's car and Ann followed. As we drove, I tried to offer some support. "Karen, for what it's worth, you did the classy thing by not yelling, screaming, crying, or causing a scene."

Instead of going back to Karen's home, we ended up at one of her favorite restaurants where we had dinner and drinks and talked about her next move. We could tell Karen was rapidly on her way to total amnesia. The shock and relief were overwhelming her. Her biggest concern was for her financial security. I told her we had a little recording that might keep Jeff's feet planted firmly on the ground.

Karen suspected that Jeff would hear from Jennifer before the evening was over and wouldn't go home. "He'll have to go somewhere to form his game plan and regain his composure. And he's probably turned everything around so it's all my fault!"

"You may want to have a lawyer draw up some preliminary agreement papers for leverage," I suggested.

When we finally took Karen home it was late and Jeff's car wasn't in the garage. Inside, the telephone message light was flashing. One of the messages was from Jeff. He was obviously in tears. He assured her it was just this one time. He said they'd had too much to drink and it didn't mean a thing.

"I'll do anything to make it up to you. I love you, Babe!"

Another message was from Karen's son. He was calling from college. "What's going on, Mom? Dad called tonight. He was crying and said you're divorcing him." Karen was fuming. "Why did that bastard have to bring Tony into this mess?"

"Probably because he's desperate and doesn't want to lose you," I suggested. "He's grabbing at anything and everything to keep you from leaving him."

"Well, what do I do now?" she asked.

What could we say? This was her decision and hers alone. However, we had an idea that might work if Jeff was truly serious about keeping his family together … and if Karen was willing to give him another chance. We told her to have him back up his promises with a financial commitment, in writing, legal and binding. He was to guarantee Karen full ownership of the homes in Bel Aire and Aspen, the cars, and any other major financial assets they had, if he should ever be caught with another woman again.

"Just let your fingers do the walking under 'A' for an attorney, if you don't already know one."

Karen asked if we'd like to spend the night in the guestroom, but we declined. She thanked us and we left.

A few months later we heard from Karen. Jeff was staying and he had signed over their assets. Karen was feeling pretty good about herself and even had a little nip and tuck here and there to keep her spirits up. She said they were seeing a marriage counselor, hashing out their differences, and trying to learn to love and trust one another again.

18

Run, Forrest! Run!

Denise, a woman in her mid-forties and the mother of two teenagers, had read about my services in a magazine and decided to call. She was quite sure her fifty-year-old husband, Chad, had met someone else. She had tried to talk with him about her suspicions, but he would either get mad or ignore her. She was becoming concerned about her future.

"I need proof," she said, "but surveillance is out of the question as he's in charge of a large construction company in the Simi Valley."

I asked Denise what had prompted her suspicions.

"I've noticed he listens to his voice mail, and then immediately makes some excuse to go to the store or someplace. I just know if I could listen to the messages, I'd be able to find out what's going on. Is there any way at all for me to get his voice mail number and password?"

I told Denise her request wasn't out of the ordinary, and I was quite sure there was electronic equipment available to help her. I met with Denise the next day and showed her some brochures of recorders that not only recorded from a telephone, but also deciphered the DTMF tones—the distinctive sounds the phone makes when you dial each number. Without hesitation, Denise ordered one of these little wonders of the electronic age and set it up to intercept the calls on her husband's telephone. The following is her account of what happened.

After setting up the device, she immediately played back the tones Chad had dialed and the recorder displayed a combination of numbers— 4234565-2134-1-3. This indicated he had called 423-4565, and after the voicemail system answered, he entered 2134—his four-digit password. To listen to his messages, he dialed 1, and after he listened to them, he dialed 3 to erase them.

Armed with Chad's voice mail number and password, Denise was able to call in and listen directly to his voice mail messages. Within three days, she discovered who the other woman was, as well as where and when they met.

Denise gave her husband some time to be straight with her, but when several months passed and he never did, she emptied all the money out of their joint accounts. She then placed a call to the other woman's husband, Richard, at work (he was also in construction). She told him where and when his wife and Chad were planning their next rendezvous and invited him to meet her there. Unbeknownst to Denise, Richard was a very large man with an explosive temper.

Denise waited at the motel where her husband and Richard's wife, Sandra, were to meet. She wasn't sure if Richard would show up, but she was prepared to confront the lovebirds herself. Suddenly, in a cloud of gravel, a large pickup truck slid into the motor lodge parking lot and a lumberjack of a man crawled out and headed straight for Room 103. Denise saw that Richard was considerably younger than Chad, and much bigger! She felt a twinge of fear. It was obvious Richard was out of control, and she wasn't sure what was going to happen.

As soon as Richard arrived at the room, he kicked open the door. Someone screamed, and then she heard loud yelling. The next thing she knew, a naked Chad came flying out the door, running for his life, with Richard right behind him! Denise's emotions ran the gamut from absolute fear for Chad's safety to total hysterics as she watched him streaking through the motor lodge parking lot. She could see faces peering out room windows and people opening doors to see what was going on. She never realized how fast Chad could run!

She started up her car and honked the car horn as she passed Chad in his flight. Complete terror was etched on his face and he begged her to stop the car so he could get in. She just waved at him and slowly continued to drive alongside of him. After about a mile, she finally let him get in the car. Richard had stopped several blocks back.

Denise decided not to divorce Chad. The pitiful jerk was so humiliated that he quit his job and made plans to move to a small community. She told me a day doesn't go by that he doesn't apologize for his behavior and swears he'll do anything if she'll just stay with him. All the assets are in her name and she says if he ever cheats on her again, she going to claim every one of them.

The one thing she never told Chad was about the little electronic wonder she used to catch him. To this day, he thinks it was all Richard's doing.

19

From Dud
to Dude

Mike was a tall, gray-haired, handsome executive at the pinnacle of his career. He was also well into his forties with a beautiful new home, a new sports car, and an old wife. Got the picture?

You see, the problem was that the more he acquired new shit, the more his wife of 18 years became old shit. Mike was hit on every day by the "wannabe new wife" who was dreaming of living in a big house and driving a new sports car. This guy would provide plenty of security after all of these years of toil and maturing ... and I mean "maturing."

You see, a lot of husbands feel they need a shapely young girlfriend to not only reflect their new lifestyle but to boost their fragile egos. Yes, I'm afraid that many men who cheat on their wives feel they have earned the right to regress back to their "getting laid" look. They were hard-working guys who had a vision of future greatness. However, somewhere along their way down the road to success they found themselves becoming more and more self-indulgent. It's a pity so many men have such fragile egos that they need to ruin such great partnerships with the woman who helped them get to the top.

Mike was in his mid 40's and a top supervisor of a large corporation. His wife of 18 years, Julie, had managed to put Mike through college, raise three children and keep a nice home. She was a "fox" when Mike married her back in the 70s, a petite wisp of a woman with sandy blonde hair and an hourglass figure. In the 90s she's looked a little tired and had a more rounded figure. She had that "comfy look" about her. Julie was a sweet, loving mother, and a loving and devoted wife to Mike, which made it all the more difficult for her to meet with me.

"I pray that this is all in my imagination," she began, "but I'm concerned that my husband, Mike, is having an affair. I just can't believe he would do that after all we have meant to each other."

"And what have you meant to each other?" I asked.

"Well, I've worked very hard to send him through school, and managed the house and children for all these years. I have been with him through thick and thin. And now, all of a sudden, when business is great and he's had one promotion after another, I feel that he is replacing me with a newer model. It hurts so much. What will I do, where will I go? I'm too old to start all over again." The tears escaped down her cheeks.

Damn, I wished I hadn't asked her that question. I hate it when women cry.

"Okay, try to relax," I said as I passed her the tissue box. "What makes you so sure he's having an affair?"

"He's coming home late. He's argumentative with me over really trivial things. I can't seem to satisfy him, no matter how hard I try. I get these damn phone calls about 10 minutes before he arrives home and I know someone is on the other end, but they won't talk. They just listen to me asking over and over again, 'Who is this?'"

"Has your husband changed his wardrobe lately?"

"Yes, for a matter fact, he has. He's been wearing cowboy boots, Levi's and even a cowboy hat."

I wondered if he'd been hitting the local line-dance circuit, but decided not to ask right now. I told Julie that it seems to fit a pattern men have while having an affair. Julie replied that she needed some very good proof because he would never admit to anything. I advised Julie that she must take these next few weeks to gather her thoughts about what she intends to do if her worst nightmare were to come true, and I asked her to call me if she suspected that her husband might be going out in his western attire.

I went home and told Ann that we'd have to get ourselves outfitted for some country western style surveillance. Thanks to a little stop in Las Vegas during another case (and that's another book), I had a pair of cowboy boots, a pearl-button shirt, blue jeans, and even an authentic cowboy hat. I wore it in Las Vegas and home on the plane, but it lost its allure once I hit the San Francisco freeway. Ann would just doll herself up in a countrified skirt and dancing shoes. At least it wasn't going to amount to a costly shopping excursion!

"Are you're taking me dancing?" said my pretty little wife, hopefully.

"I'm taking y'all out on surveillance," I replied in my best Texas twang, "as soon as our new client calls."

"And then are you going to take me dancing?"

"What's with you and dancing?"

"Well, I thought while we were there we could dance too!"

"No! You dance and I videotape y'all on the dance floor with our guy in the background. Got it?"

"Yep, sure do pardner!" Ann laughed as she did a little foot stomping jig in the middle of the room. Now that we had that straight, all we needed was to wait for the phone call. Friday night was just three days away; and if Mike was going, it would probably be either Friday or Saturday.

Wrong! I received a call from Julie early Wednesday evening.

"Greg, this is Julie! Mike called me from his office a few minutes ago and told me he was going out tonight with the guys from work. He asked if I would wash his pearl button shirt. He said he'd be leaving at eight. Can you tail him?"

"Sure!" I replied. "Annie, get your dancing shoes on ... we're going out!"

We sure did look good, me and the Mrs. ... wished I had me one of them big silver belt buckles.

I packed up the low light video camera, extra batteries, and a blank videotape. I brought my audio transmitter and receiver just in case I came close enough to catch our guy talking to his lady friend.

We arrived at Julie's home. Ann was driving the Mercedes and I was driving the Ford Aerostar. Ann parked on the street that crosses in front of the court and I parked on the main thoroughfare. We'd round up our cowboy coming or going, north or south. Ann and I checked our two-way radio transmission. The sound was clear.

At 8:20 p.m. I heard Ann's voice over the radio, "He's pulled out of the garage, driving a black 1995 BMW and heading towards you."

I waited for him to commit to a direction and radioed to Ann that he was heading south on 680 and 580 towards Livermore. Ann confirmed and we followed at a safe distance. Before long, I put myself a few car lengths ahead of Mike while Ann remained behind and one lane over. We knew that if he decided to get off the freeway he would make his move to our lanes.

As we approached Pleasanton, Ann noticed that our guy was changing lanes as though he might be getting ready to take one of the exists. She warned me over the radio so that I could slow down and let him pass me, which he did, and then he pulled in front of me. He exited the freeway at Sunol Blvd. and headed east.

Ann and I followed him to a large new home located in the Ruby Hills Development off Vineyard Ave. He had to stop at a security station in order to get through. We knew we had to act fast or we would loose him. I drove up to the security station and informed the security guard that I was an investigator and needed access, along with the vehicle behind me. I showed him my credentials and he lifted the gate. We both drove through and caught up to Mike, who had driven along the roadway bordering the golf course and into a court.

We found his vehicle parked in the driveway of a small home with children's toys scattered all over the front lawn. We video recorded the home with Mike's car parked in the driveway. I reached into the back seat of my surveillance van and pulled out my laptop computer. I ran the ownership of the property and found that is was listed to a John and Helen Casper. I then ran the name of Casper in Alameda County to see if they had any civil actions such as a divorce. *Voila!* Helen divorced John approximately eight months ago.

The setting sun was a blessing; we didn't want to cause suspicion among the neighbors. I walked around the home from a respectable distance, hoping to find an opened window that would reveal what the occupants were up to—and through which I could videotape! The community had a wall around the backyards, and the distance from the wall to the windows was considerable. Plus, you don't want to enter onto private property without an invitation.

We were confident they would give us the video we needed before the night was through. At 9:30, a young girl came to the door and was asked to come in. We figured she was probably the baby-sitter. Moments later "our hero" and a woman we believed to be Helen left in her vehicle, leaving Mike's car on the other side of the driveway. It was easy following Helen, a tall redhead dressed in cowgirl duds, and we followed them towards Livermore.

They pulled up to a country western nightclub and parked in the back. Ann "shot" them as they entered hand-in-hand into the club. I parked the van on the street and Ann parked her car in the back with a view of Helen's red Jeep. Then we met in front of the club and moseyed on in. We walked around the bar and dance floor until we spotted Mike and Helen standing with four other couples.

Ann wondered aloud if these people knew Julie and were covering up for Mike. I just said that she shouldn't worry her pretty little head about such things, and to go find herself some overweight, ugly cowboy to dance with while I videotaped her, with Mike and Helen in the background. It was easier than I thought. There were a number of people with camera's taking film or video of the dancers. It was amateur night for the new cowpokes and their ladies. They were learning how to line dance and Mike was a novice!

My thoughts wandered to Julie. She would have enjoyed the chance to learn line dancing with her hubby. Oh well, I think Mike will be learning some other steps in the not too distant future.

Everyone was having fun, including Ann, who was dancing with the group Mike was in. What really added to the entertainment was when a friend of Mike's asked Ann if she would like to join them. The guy started buying Ann drinks and dancing with her, and introduced her to Mike and Helen. Soon they were all connected at the hip. Ann excused herself and headed towards the lady's room, gesturing to me to follow. She asked me to get the transmitter from the van and give it to her so we could record Mike and Helen.

I bolted out to the van and came back with a transmitter and mini recorder, and Ann placed it in her handbag. Ann returned to the group and asked Helen to watch her handbag for a moment. I was on the other side of the room, monitoring their conversation—which, by the way, was taking place in public, where the expectation for privacy is a big zero! Extramarital lovers tend to talk a lot about their future. Mike told Helen that it wouldn't be long before the children would be 18 and he wouldn't have to pay child support. In the meantime, he was going to persuade Julie to get back into school or some sort of training program, without letting on that the ultimate goal was teaching her to be self-supporting. He also told Helen about his plans to hide most of the assets so he wouldn't go broke when he gave Julie her walking papers.

Helen confided that she had spent the last three years of her marriage hiding assets from her ungrateful husband and that Mike would be wise to do the same. The twosome continued to plot and plan. However, I knew from past experience that Mike had no such plans to dump Julie ... not in a million years. All of Mike's scheming, how he planned to divorce Julie once certain conditions had been met, is an old line philandering men have used to keep their lovers on the hook. The old standbys—waiting for the children to grow up, waiting for their wife to become self-sufficient, or waiting for a financial matter to get cleaned up. Men know new wives don't want to be burdened with any financial problems from the prior marriage.

By midnight, I'd noticed that Mike hadn't used a phone to call his wife so she wouldn't worry. The group looked like it was about to split up. Ken, or as I referred to him, "Mr. Jeans So Tight, It's a Miracle He Can Move ... but it's okay because his gut's hanging over his silver belt buckle"—the same guy who's been dancing with my wife all night—asked for her phone number! I would have loved to hear that conversation! I just hoped she told him about the jealous man she's married to ... a real raving lunatic.

I hightailed it to the parking lot. My van was the one vehicle that wasn't seen at either the club or Helen's home, so I raced back to Helen's and set up the camera on the tripod to hopefully capture some fond embraces in the driveway. A few minutes later, Ann radioed to let me know that the lovebirds were kissing all the way home and were now passing through the security gate.

I sank down behind the seat as the Jeep pulled around the corner and up the driveway. Mike opened the driver's side door, walked around the front of the Jeep, and opened the passenger door for Helen. He then pressed her up against the right fender of the Jeep. Thanks to state-of-the-art technology enabling my video camera to capture every inch of groping and squeezing under the dim streetlight, there would be no doubt in my client's mind; this little outing would confirm her suspicions. And were those two going at it! His hand was up her dress and down her dress, and her hands were all over his butt. I was tempted to jump out of the van and turn the hose on them. This videotape would be all Julie needed to confirm her suspicions. Mike walked Helen to the front door with his hand on the small of her back and slipping down over the curve of her hip. He left Helen at the door and returned to his car for the ride home. Since Ann and I were going that way anyway, we thought it would be nice to make sure he went straight home.

Surprise! Mike turned off in Dublin and drove to a small tract home off of Tamarack. He pulled up to the driveway and walked to the front door of the home. A young woman came to the door, talked to Mike for a minute and let him in!

Ann and I bolted out of our vehicles. Ann checked the front of the home while I looked over the fence at the rear. I noticed a bedroom light in the back bedroom and a silhouette of two people moving around. The lights went out. I headed toward the front of the house and instead found Ann standing right next to me recording the two images on the curtain. I told Ann that she should go home and get some sleep and I would catch Mike leaving later in the morning.

By 2:40 a.m., I noticed a light go on in the living room. Mike stepped out from the front door with a young brunette behind him. He hesitated and they talked for a moment. Mike put his left arm around the young woman's neck, and his right hand found its way down the inside of her robe. The video camera was rolling.

He returned to his BMW, and I assumed that he was really going to go home this time. I certainly intended to go home. Ann was still awake, and we watched the video. Not just one woman, but two! This is about the best you can do when attempting to catch a spouse or "significant other" cheating, other than catching them actually "doing it."

After Ann and I reviewed the tapes with Julie, she needed a shoulder to cry on and a woman to talk to. I was the shoulder, and Ann was the sympathetic ear. I gave Julie my standard words of encouragement. The subject of "getting even" inevitably came up. I reminded Julie not to break any laws or undermine her own security in an overzealous attempt to make life miserable for the lying bag of shit. I was hoping that my words of wisdom weren't going in one ear and out the other. Julie was utterly disappointed, disgusted, and out for blood!

I told Julie to keep in touch and if she ever needed a friend to bounce her feelings off of, to just call ... any time. And she did ... about five months later. Julie had been on a wonderful cruise, had lost 25 lbs., had a makeover, bought lots of new expensive clothes, and "Studley Doright" had financed the whole experience. She didn't tell him about the audio and videotapes! She just added them to her collection of information about his liquid assets, which she began to spend lavishly on herself and the children. Mike went out of town and Julie held a garage sale, selling all sorts of worthless junk; his fishing tackle, bowling ball, his prized collection of baseball cards, old coins, and those ridiculous cowboy boots.

Julie was divorcing Mike now that he'd returned from his "business" trip. Mike knew he'd been caught! But we were correct about Mike. He didn't want to lose Julie, but he didn't have that choice anymore. Julie was looking good ... much better than the fillies we saw him with that night. And was she's feeling good too. She's slim, tan and single. Julie said she'd been thinking of taking dancing lessons the first chance she got ... after the summer in Europe.

20

House
For Sale

The most difficult cases we work on are those dealing with real estate agents. They have an unlimited time frame to cheat in, and they have an abundance of locales to choose from, with the extra perk of no motel bills.

John fell madly in love with Beth. They were both real estate agents; and between the two of them, they had a number of vacant properties at their disposal: town homes, condominiums, and a nice variety of single-family residences. They each had their exclusive listings, and anyone who wants to see one of their homes would be required to contact either John or Beth for a "walk through."

Now let's say my client, Peggy, is married to John. John has a furnished condominium on the market. He calls Beth, "Hey Babe, meet at the condo on Silver Lake." Beth is on the way, and no one at the office thinks anything of it. After all, it's her business to be ready to show a home at a moment's notice.

As a private eye, your job is to watch John all day to see where he goes and whom he's meeting with. John meets Beth, and until you know the names of the players and what their game is, she could be just any prospective homebuyer.

This is where I have to take notes of every detail, a full description of the woman, including a description of her car. I'm developing a pattern of John's activities. You can begin to imagine how difficult this assignment is going to be. Our lovebirds go to properties she lists and properties he lists. I'll never know where they're going next. Then, of course, they could be seeing legitimate clients, and you spend the rest of the week following him without him becoming suspicious.

There's one point in our favor. Realtors, like physicians, lawyers, and other business professionals, must stay in communication with their offices.

Most of you have a cellphone. Do you realize that those conversations are not private? Those words of love float over the airwaves, just like the local radio station, and with the right equipment, yours truly can pick up every word. And that's how we caught John and Beth. We had John's cell phone number, so all we had to do was program his number into our scanning device. Every time his phone rang, the conversation would come through loud and clear. It was then recorded ... every "Darling, Honey, Sweetie," as well as the time and place of their next rendezvous.

We hit paydirt the second day out. John placed a call from his car to Beth's answering machine that he would meet her at the Silver Lake Condo by 2:00 p.m. This knowledge would give us time to place suction devices on the windows of the bedrooms to monitor the sound emanating from each room using a multiple scanning unit.

John showed up first, carrying a brown bag in his right hand. John reminded me of Sam Malone (Ted Danson) in *"Cheers,"* except this guy had blond hair. But he had Sam's strut and the voice was similar. Beth showed up about 20 minutes later, dressed in a short black skirt, black sweater, black nylons, high heels, and a red blazer. Ann was operating the audio scanner while I videotaped. Ann located the frequency that placed them in the master bedroom, and we heard John pouring something that fizzled. I then plugged the line from the scanner into the video camera "in" port, which allowed me to record the outside of the house, John's and Beth's cars parked in front, and the moans and groans from the master bedroom. They really surprised Ann and me as we sat through five non-stop orgasms. I asked Ann if she thought Beth was faking. Regardless of whether or not Beth was faking her moments of ecstasy, I was sure John was more than spent.

"Trust me, he's done," I instructed, "and there's no point in following him around for the rest of the afternoon and evening. We should call Peggy."

As always, our man had a difficult time saying thanks to his lover for such a wonderful afternoon. Men usually use both audio and physical afterplay to keep the woman's interest. It usually goes something like: "Oh Baby, you're so wonderful! I can't bear to think of being without you in my arms for even a minute," as his hand slides up her skirt. "I can't get enough of you. Your scent drives me mad with passion." Tongue enters her mouth as left hand messages between her legs. "I love you," and he walks her to her car, patting her ass one last time. "Bye, Baby. I'll miss you."

She says, "I'll miss you too!" and drives off thinking, "I'm glad it was fun for you, Tarzan, but if it wouldn't hurt your fragile male ego too much, I'd like to enjoy it too."

In other words, "I should have an Academy Award for that performance!"

This is efficiency at its best thanks to modern technology. Our job is wrapped up and we present Peggy with film at six.

21

The Mistress

I thought I had seen it all, but this one surprised me.

It was early fall and I received a call. The voice was that of a well-educated young woman. Diane wanted to talk to me because her experience with other investigators had been less than satisfactory. I agreed to meet her at the Brass Door in San Ramon. The owner and I go back to our high school days in Danville. I knew Danny would find an inconspicuous place for my client to meet with me. Diane was there when I arrived and Danny seated us in a remote corner.

Diane told me she had been in love with Ted for just over five years. He had promised to marry her as soon as his children left home for college.

"I can assume Ted is married?" I asked.

"Yes," Diane confessed. "He's married and I'm afraid I've been a fool to believe him all this time. He keeps saying we'll

179

be together soon and for always. I can't believe I've been so naive. The reason I need your help is because Ted has not been coming around as much lately. I know it's not his wife who is occupying his time because he say he abhors being with her."

Diane went on to explain their relationship.

"Ted and I met five years ago while I was working on my master's degree at San Francisco State. I met him through one of those work projects where students learn what it's like to work for different kinds of companies. Ted showed up at one of my classes. He looked so incredibly handsome in a three-piece suit, a little gray at the temples, and my first thought was how I would like to marry a man like Ted. Ted was powerful and confident. I felt like a teenager, just melting whenever I thought of him."

"Ted noticed my infatuation and invited me to dinner in the city. I was overwhelmed by the beautiful luxury car that he drove and the exquisite restaurant we went to. It was like a Cinderella story, except for one thing. Ted said he had been unhappily married for 25 years to a control freak who had gained 50 lbs. and was down on herself so much that she had destroyed any love they once had for each other.

"Ted told me he was prepared to get a divorce as soon as the children left for college. Our youngest is in her junior year in high school. That meant just two years and he would have freedom. He professed his unending love for me, and I felt that I was the luckiest woman on earth to find such a loving, charming man to spend my life with. Ted asked if I would be willing to wait for him, and I said I'd wait forever, but now I'm thinking it just may be forever!

"He told me he'd buy me a condominium, and all I had to do was be there for him during those difficult two years. I thought the time would fly; we would get married and live happily ever after. Wrong! The two years went by fast enough and then the excuses began. First, a divorce before Doris' operation would spell financial ruin. Ted wanted to send her back to school so she could gain some career skills, which would substantially reduce his spousal support payment. Then it was the needs of the children. Then it was his mother-in-law's illness, or an upcoming event that he just had to be there for Doris. Five years later, I think Ted is cheating on me and all I have to show for my devotion is age, no job prospects and no income other than what he pays me per month. And that will amount to nothing if he replaces me with someone else. I need you to follow Ted. I want to know if he's seeing another woman."

The other investigators Diane had called didn't offer much moral support. Their position boiled down to the fact that Diane didn't have much money to spend on hourly surveillance efforts, and that this was the typical "other woman" finding out what 99% of women in her position learn sooner or later. Diane was hurting … really hurting. I thought we might be able to put her mind at ease quickly by determining who Ted was seeing, if anyone, and then letting Diane get her life on track as quickly as possible, with or without Ted.

"Do you have a picture of Ted?" I asked. "I'll also need a description of his car, his home and business addresses, telephone numbers, and anything else you can tell me about his daily habits."

Ted had a business meeting the next day at corporate offices located at Bishop Ranch Business Park. Ann and I were waiting in the parking lot. Ted's 1994 silver Mercedes Benz 300 SL was nearby.

"Mobile one to mobile two, do you read?"

"This is mobile two! What do you want?" Ann replied.

"I want to know where you're located."

"If you're such a hot private eye, come on and find me!"

I feel like Rodney Dangerfield ... no respect! This is one of the drawbacks of working with your spouse. A real employee would never treat me like this. Well, at least not for the first week or so, until they get to know me.

A masculine voice came over the mobile radio, "Mobile one this is mobile three. Do you have a surveillance going on in the Ma Bell parking lot?"

"That's a Roger three!" I recognized Bert's voice. "Who are you covering Bert?"

"A guy named Ken, a cheating husband."

"One to three, what parking lot is he in?"

"Ma Bell's. The same one you're in," Bert replied.

"What a coincidence. What's your subject driving, three? " A silver Mercedes Benz 300 SL."

There was a moment of radio silence. I asked the big question, "Bert, could it be we're tailing the same guy?"

"Sure sounds like it."

"Bert, I don't remember setting up your surveillance."

"You didn't," Bert replied. "The call came in yesterday and I booked it for today. The client's name is Doris and she thinks her husband is having an affair."

"Ann and I are working for his mistress and you're working for his wife."

"Come back one! Did you say you're working for his mistress?"

"That's right," Bert answered.

"That's a big ten four. I ran the 300 SL through the DMV, and the registered owner is Theodore Crame. Your client says her husband's name is Ken?"

"This is one of those conflict of interest cases that just can't be helped. Let's play it like this. We'll blanket this guy and hope he dates someone other than my client. That way we can send each client a videotape with Ted, or Ken, or whatever his name is, to our prospective clients and they won't have to know about each other."

"Sounds good to me. His wife is just trying to protect his identify if her suspicions are wrong."

"Ann, are you by?"

"Yeah. What do you want know?"

"Where are you located?"

"Back to that same old question. Look towards the entrance to Ma Bell's. See that gorgeous girl sitting just inside the entrance? Now look at her with your binoculars."

I looked and there was my Annie smiling, remote in her purse, and looking so smug. I could hear Bert laughing over the radio. "Hey, Greg, can you top that?"

What was so funny was you needed a pass card to gain entrance. While Bert and I were watching the car, Ann had managed to sweet talk herself past the security gate and plant herself in an ideal position to see the subject when he left. An hour and a half passed. We noticed Ann going into the building Ted was in. A few minutes later she came back, carrying apple juice and a sandwich. We were more than a little envious since it was more than a little past our lunchtime.

As Ann was finishing her lunch, Ted came out of the building and headed for his car. Ann tossed her lunch bag in the garbage and hopped into her car, following Ted from a distance and giving us a blow-by-blow description of Ted's travel plans. Ted did not leave by the front gate. Instead he left through a side gate that took him directly to the Marriott Hotel. Ann videotaped his stroll across the parking lot to another car. He opened the door of the green T-bird and an attractive young woman in her early twenties emerged. She was a long-legged blonde, suntanned and wearing a short skirt and light sweater. Hand-in-hand, Ted escorted her to the hotel.

I had promised to call Diane if we saw him with another woman. Diane asked me where I was and said she would be right over to confront him.

Ann and Bert walked into the Marriott while I stayed outside looking for Diane. A few minutes later, Diane pulled up in her Jeep, got out, and started walking towards the Marriott. Diane looked beautiful as she headed for the entrance.

"Hold it Diane! I can't allow you to do anything foolish. You have to let me see the contents of your purse."

"It's okay. I won't shoot the bastard. I just want him to know that it's over for me ... and his wife. I'll go right to her and tell her myself all that's been going on behind her back!"

Diane's purse had no weapons in it other than a cardboard fingernail file. Diane's clothing didn't reveal any bulges to suggest a concealed weapon. "Okay, Diane. If you need any assistance, just whistle. You do know how to whistle, don't you?"

She knew I was trying to take the edge off her frustration and anger with my Humphrey Bogart impression, and I think it helped a little.

Diane waited a few minutes, and then went to the seventh floor where Ted had taken the blonde. Ann, Bert, and I escorted Diane down the long hallway towards room 710. We all stopped to see what Diane was going to do next.

With a Hispanic accent Diane beat on the door, "Excuse me ... excuse me. I need to leave clean towels. Please open the door."

A nude Ted opened the door just enough to end up on his butt when Diane shoved the door open. Diane bolted in to the room and told the blonde, "Hi, did you know you're number 3 or number 4? You had better marry him, because he'll be available now that his wife and mistress know what he's up to."

Diane called Ted every vile name in the book while we were busy videotaping. Ted was just sitting on the floor in a daze. The blonde slipped out from under the covers and headed for the bathroom with her clothes draped over her arm. Diane let loose, "You're a son-of-a-bitch to do this! You're nothing but a coward to do this to your wife and me! You deserve what you get, you prick!"

The whole time she was yelling at Ted he kept putting his arms up as if to fend off any fists she might throw at him. She didn't take her fists from her hips, and we had one of the most entertaining videotapes a client could ask for.

As we walked down the stairs, I announced to our entourage, "The drinks are on me."

After our congratulatory toasts, we pondered the outcome of Doris's reaction to the video. We felt sorry for Doris, knowing that she would be cognizant of her husband's affairs with two women. She may not want to talk to Diane, but we imagined what she would be saying to Ted!

Diane found a job and has vowed to stay away from any man, no matter how good looking and successful, if he's married. Doris stayed with Ted, but last we heard, he's on a very short leash, at least for the time being. Doris is either holding something very precious over Teddy's head to keep him in line, or she's just turning her back on the truth and electing to live with a cheating husband rather than no husband at all.

22

Gucci

I suppose May mornings can be a bit chilly in the state of Washington. Margaret seemed to think so! This particular Sunday morning, Margaret stoked a warm fire and sat at her daughter's tea party table to ponder decisions about her future … and her husband's future too.

Margaret had called me two days earlier from her home just north of Seattle. The beautiful neighborhood boasted large Tudor style homes, manicured lawns, swimming pools, and patio umbrellas peeking over the top of the perfectly groomed hedges.

Margaret's husband, Mark, was an executive for a very well known computer company. He had a passion for $3,000 suits, Gucci shoes, silk ties, and easy women. His black Mercedes Benz sports coupe, great business, home, girlfriends, and the obligatory wife and child rounded off the list of important things in his life. Callous as this may sound, Mark never doubted that he loved his wife and daughter, but he felt that he had earned the right to have fun on the side; after all, he did supply them with a nice home and carte blanche shopping funds.

Margaret was educated, attractive, young, sweet, and doing the things a new mother should do. Margaret felt that, because she gained so much weight during her pregnancy with Megan, Mark had lost interest in her. She told me that when she needed him most, he would just leave the house and meet a friend at a bar. She felt very unattractive. She recalled attempting to cuddle Mark when she was in her eighth month of pregnancy; he told her to get away. She confided that she had cried for two days over that remark. Since Megan's birth, Mark had become more flamboyant and arrogant; and now, after two years, Margaret had decided enough was enough!

Mark had declared that he needed to spend all day Friday through early Sunday evening at a business symposium in the San Francisco Bay Area, and Margaret hired us to follow Mark to California. I told her we would need to know Mark's flight itinerary, and that it would be very difficult to follow Mark anywhere by plane without having an itinerary and more advanced notice. "However," I suggested, "my agent and I could check the airport out to see if Mark has, in fact, left Washington."

Ann and I checked out every parking lot and every parking space within the vicinity of the SeaTac Airport. I reported to Margaret that we had been unsuccessful in locating Mark's vehicle, and that I would be willing to bet big money that Mark was still in the vicinity for a weekend tryst. Margaret told me that the only woman whose phone number kept coming up on Mark's cell phone records belongs to Sue

Chin, their marriage counselor. Margaret had asked Mark to see a marriage counselor after one of their big arguments during the final days of Margaret's pregnancy. It appeared that Mark had called Ms. Chin frequently during the past two years ... even on weekends. I thought Mark might be getting more from Sue Chin than good advice, and I asked Margaret if she noticed any positive changes in Mark since he had been receiving counseling from Ms. Chin.

"No, I haven't," Margaret, confessed. "He comes home and starts these pissy little arguments with me. He starts off by sarcastically asking, 'so ... what have you done all day?' "

I would think that Sue Chin would have wanted to meet with Margaret during the past few years, but Margaret replied, "I have never met the woman. Mark just seems to be so mad at me for nothing. He still says the cruelest things."

I suggested we find out where Ms. Chin lives. Within an hour, my source called back with number breaks: cell, home and home business lines, and a residence address. Ann and I immediately drove to the residence address to find that it was an apartment building. We ran the license plates for all of the cars in her cluster of apartments and found a blue Honda registered to Susan L. Chin with the same apartment address. There was only an answering machine when we called her phone number. We tried her business number and received the following message: "Hello! You have reached Sue Chin, I'm sorry I'm not in to answer the phone. I will be out on Friday, May 11, and will return to work Monday morning. Please leave a message at the sound of the tone."

I called Margaret and told her that it appeared likely that Mark and Sue Chin were spending the weekend together and there was nothing we could do until Sunday. Early Sunday morning Ann and I decided to check out the layout of the neighborhood around Chin's apartment to determine the best vantage point for obtaining photographs without being obvious. If and when Mark brought Ms. Chin back to her apartment after their weekend getaway, we might be able to capture the caress and kiss. While driving around the corner to check the parking lot, we noticed a black Mercedes Benz parked near a back gate, and this grownup toy had Mark's license plate number on it. While idling in the rear parking lot, Ann noticed a ground floor window curtain open up sharply, revealing a nude Asian female looking towards the black Mercedes Benz. Just as suddenly a Caucasian male appeared over her shoulder looking in the same direction as the woman. Voila! It was Mark! Ann attempted to videotape them, but Ms. Chin glanced towards our vehicle and quickly pulled the curtains shut. We backed up and drove across the street. We had a view of Ms. Chin's front door and the route Mark would have to take to reach his vehicle. I called Margaret, and now we return to the beginning of this story ...

Margaret and Megan are sitting by the fire at little Megan's wooden table. Margaret answered the phone to hear me say, "Hi Margaret! Well it's all over. Mark is at Sue Chin's apartment, and she actually appeared at the window, naked, with Mark standing behind her. They are still there. What do you want us to do?"

There was complete silence until Margaret finally answered, "Can you stay there for at least an hour more?"

"Sure! But why?"

"I decided to burn all of the asshole's clothes, including his ties, shoes and baseball card collection. They're not burning very quickly, so I'm stoking the flames with his wooden model airplane collection."

I told Margaret that she shouldn't burn anything that's too valuable because the court may make her pay Mark back from her share of the proceeds. Margaret replied that she didn't give a shit about the consequences. He would be truly sorry when she got through with him! I heard some thumping in the background and asked Margaret what that sound was?

"Oh, the asshole has a collection of CD's of his favorite Italian music. I take them out of the plastic container, hide them under a blanket, and Megan hits them with a small hammer! Megan thinks it's a fun game to find the CD under the blanket when she smacks it with the hammer. We're having a grand tea party! So please let me know if the asshole moves."

Ann and I waited for approximately an hour and called Margaret back.

"How's the fire?"

"Roaring! I've smothered the fire a few times by putting too many suits on top but I have it down to an art now."

Thump, thump.

"I hear Megan is still bounding away."

"Well, he had over two hundred CD's. It takes time to remove a CD from its plastic holder, and Megan gives it a few good whacks, we put the pieces back in the holder, and return it to the CD display case."

An hour later we received a call from Margaret. I asked Margaret what she planned to do now.

"I really don't know. Wait until he comes home, I guess."

"If you really want to ruin his day, why don't you call him?"

"What good will that do?"

I assured Margaret that a phone call would certainly take the starch out of his rubber band.

"You know, you're right! I'll call now and you can video-tape him leaving her place."

A few minutes later Margaret called us back and was laughing uncontrollably. Margaret said that when the phone was answered by Sue Chin all she said was, "Put Mark on. I'm his wife." The next thing Margaret heard was a feminine Asian voice screaming, "You lied to me! You bastard! You didn't tell me you're married!" In the background was Mark's frantic voice yelling, "Stop hitting me with that thing!"

A few moments later, Mark emerged from Ms. Chin's residence carrying two small suitcases. He started walking towards us, but then veered to the left in the direction of his car. We took a sigh of relief and continued to videotape his journey. Mark looked as though he was going to his own funeral. The arrogant attitude had certainly disappeared.

I don't know if Margaret and Mark were able to save their marriage, but they were finally at a place to begin building a new life, together or apart. Thump! Thump!

23

"It's
Showtime!"

I consider myself to be a friendly, middle-aged, teddy-bear sort of a guy who appreciates women and hates to see them being mistreated. I was hoping this was what Susan saw in me, because she appeared to be in the grip of some unnerving emotion. At first glance, she seemed to have it all together. She was about 40, tall and trim, friendly brown eyes, and short stylish hair. Her jade green dress was very becoming and she had all the right accessories. But she was clutching her purse as though it was her lifeline.

She glanced at me keenly. Then taking a deep breath, she made the plunge. "Alan, my husband, is letting everything just fall apart. He's not paying our bills on time and he's letting the cars and the house go. Everything needs repairs, but he says we don't have the money."

I nodded knowingly. These were the classic signs of a man squirreling money away. Susan said Alan was a 47-year-old, self-made man with his own financial services corporation, complete with tax-deductible yacht and private plane. She described him as a thin, mild-mannered accountant, about six feet tall, with thinning brown hair. He normally wore conservative business clothes, fitting the image of the typical successful businessman. They had been married for 12 years, and had an 11-year-old son and a 10-year-old daughter. Her role was to manage the children and household, a 15-room home, and to entertain business clients.

I've listened to enough women, my wife included, to know that "homemaker" is a full-time occupation. Susan felt she had done her job well and created a gracious home with healthy kids, yet she knew something was wrong with the marriage. With tears in her eyes, she related her story.

Two years earlier, Alan had an affair. Susan had found out, but they patched things up when Alan promised to give up his 26-year-old playmate and behave himself. She wanted to believe his repentance was real, but her anguish at learning the man she loved had been lying to her was almost unbearable. She felt she had done everything a wife was supposed to do; tended the home, kept fit, communicated with his relatives, learned his moods, and tried to meet his needs. The affair had been a total betrayal.

Like many women, she blamed herself for getting too involved with the kids and promised herself she would spend more time doing her husband's favorite things. Perhaps it would be all right. And for a while it was. Business was good and their life seemed to be back to normal.

Then a year ago, Alan began to change. He threw away his glasses and got contact lenses (another classic sign). He spent more time on his appearance and started wearing trendy clothes. When he left on "business trips" to Santa Barbara, he now wore upscale cotton slacks and loafers instead of his usual conservative suits.

More ominously, Alan began complaining that his business was losing money. He insisted that they cut back on everything—no more vacations in Mexico, no more elaborate dinner parties, no more carefree shopping trips to the better suburban malls. Even the reasonable and necessary expense of repairing the roof on their house was more than they could afford, according to Alan. He took away Susan's credit cards, saying they couldn't afford to charge anything.

At first, Susan tried to believe Alan and be supportive during these hard times. But his decisions made her wonder. Supposedly, they did not have money to fix their cars or their home, but he kept his 60-foot yacht and his twin-engine private plane. Each was worth hundreds of thousands of dollars, more than enough to repair the roof and pay normal living expenses. Susan tried to tell herself it was just a business downturn, and that it would be silly to unload the boat and plane at a loss just when business might pick up at any moment. But the odd pattern continued and became hard to ignore. Then one day, when opening the mail, Susan found credit card receipts for charges of flowers and jewelry—gifts she had never received.

Sadly, Susan realized he was cheating again. This time, though, she could not forgive and forget, and decided to get a divorce. But with that decision came another worry. What about her financial situation? She had been a homemaker for 12 years. How would she make a living? Who would support the children, if Alan's business was in such sad shape? But maybe, she thought, his business was not in such bad shape after all. She decided to get some help.

That's where I came in. I told Susan if her husband was involved with another woman and planning to leave her, he might be hiding assets. When a man is cheating and contemplating divorce, he starts to set up his next home by gradually squirreling away cash and other valuables, from gems to baseball cards. If he's clever, the wife never notices anything is missing. Even if she does suspect something, finding the assets is a difficult and often fruitless task.

I asked Susan what she knew about Alan's business affairs and alleged financial problems. She told me he was very secretive. "He says I might say something to give his competitor an edge"

A likely story! I wondered how long she had bought this line. How often, when lunching with her women friends, had she smiled and changed the subject to avoid discussing family finances?

"Do you believe that?" I asked.

"Not any more," she said dryly. "I don't believe anything he says now."

"We need to take a look at that office," I said, "because there's something there he doesn't want you to see."

"You mean ... break in?" she asked, wide-eyed at the suggestion.

"Think about it. It's your money, too."

I closed the conversation on this suspenseful note, leaving her with something dramatic to ponder. A month later, Susan called. We met at a small café in San Francisco. Again, she was perfectly dressed, poised and charming. As we sipped our iced cappuccinos, I couldn't imagine why anyone would want to cheat on her.

She looked me in the eye. I could tell she had made up her mind. "I've decided I want you to get into my husband's office," she said.

I told her she would have to accompany me. She gave me a look of total disbelief. I quietly explained to her that, under California law, his office was community property so she could legally go in whenever she liked. On this visit, I would accompany her as her "guest."

I could tell she was thinking it over. In a few moments, she quickly accepted the idea of taking an active part in her own rescue, put down her cup, and wrote a check retaining me for my services. We planned our strategy.

A week later, at ten o'clock on a Friday night, we were sitting in my car outside Alan's office waiting for a good moment to "break in." Legal as our entry might be, we didn't want to be observed. It would ruin our plan. Susan needed to get information without letting her husband know she was up to something, or else he might hide other things. The last thing we wanted was to be found in his office!

Susan had seen too many crime movies and came dressed like a Hollywood burglar. She wore form-fitting black slacks, a tight black cotton turtleneck sweater, black calfskin gloves, a black beret, and for some reason, black high heels. A very attractive outfit, albeit somewhat impractical. On the other hand, my assistant, Steve, and I wore jeans, work shirts, and running shoes—more the "casual break-in" look, designed to be unobtrusive. You really don't want to look like a burglar when breaking into someone's office!

Susan giggled with anticipation and nervousness. She had probably never done anything naughty in her life. Steve and I were nervous, too, but for a different reason. During our many hours of waiting at various stakeouts, we had spent more than a few minutes imagining how things could go wrong. Getting shot by a gun-happy security guard, or being confronted by the local police, or getting surprised by the very husband we were investigating, was not what we wanted. Steve and I kept up the small talk to keep our minds occupied.

After the guards went by on their rounds, Susan and I would have a two-minute window of time to run across the lot, pick the front door, race to Alan's office, pick that lock, get in, and close the door. Steve would stay in the car, monitor the guard's activities, and keep in touch with me through our walkie-talkies.

After a two-hour wait, we got our chance. "Put on your gloves," I told Susan as I put on mine. "Watch for my signal and then follow me. It's show time!"

I got out of the car, closing the door quietly. In these situations, even the slightest sound seems like a thunderclap. I ran up to the front door and raked a thin lock pick over the tumblers in the lock. My palms were sweating. I had the door open in about 30 seconds—but under these circumstances, 30 seconds felt like an eternity.

I waved to Susan. She ran from the car, her high heels clattering on the pavement. I winced at every clatter. But she reached the door without being discovered and we went upstairs to her husband's office. Of course I closed the front door so that from outside everything would seem normal.

Alan had placed good locks on his office door, and I could hear my heart pounding as I worked the pick over the lock's tumblers. You have to stay focused to pick a lock. If your mind wanders, you'll miss a tumbler and be back to square one. It's delicate work and it can't be hurried.

After a few minutes, the locks were open. It's a great feeling, a real rush when you crack a lock. You feel like a genius that should get an award. "And for outstanding service to a client in breaking and entering ... "

Since there were no exterior windows from Alan's office, we were able to turn on the interior lights. I rolled my coat up and placed it at the bottom of the door to prevent any light from escaping. His five-room office was huge, as big as some homes I'd seen. But his tastes didn't impress me. The rooms were filled with early American rental furniture, overstuffed, expensive, and tacky. The paintings on the walls were real enough. They were very modern; you could have hung them sideways and no one would have known the difference. For his personal comfort, Alan had installed a hot tub, sauna, and wet bar. Five gray metal filing cabinets, all locked, stood along one wall. I had them open in less than two minutes and motioned to Susan to begin searching them while I picked the locks on his desk drawers. We were both jumpy. No matter how "expert" you may be or how legal your right to be in a place, no detective wants to be caught. Every click and every scrape is magnified. Time slows down. Everything seems to take too long.

We worked quickly and quietly. As we went, we copied anything that looked interesting on the office copier, ironically using Alan's own machine to trap him. Susan was on her hands and knees looking through the files in the bottom drawer when I found the marital equivalent of a smoking gun.

It was a plain brown manila file. On its tab in bold letters, the label read "DIVORCE SUSAN." I could only imagine the cool, calculating cruelty of this man, writing down his plan to leave and impoverish his wife and children, filed next to his client folders and operations manuals.

According to the file, he had meticulously planned this move for over a year. He was making credit card payments late, stopped making repairs to the house, and delayed routine car maintenance. He collected gold bars, Krugerrand coins, gems, and cash. Assets were hidden in his brother's name, to be collected after the divorce was final. When he had completed his agenda, he would divorce Susan, leaving her and his children as close to broke as possible.

I had never met Alan, but after reading the "DIVORCE SUSAN" file, I despised him. No one is perfect, and maybe there had been stresses in the marriage, but nothing justified such a cruel, heartless plot. Susan didn't deserve to be abused, and I was glad I'd be able to help her deal with this creep.

I called Susan over. "Sit down before you look at this," I said, and handed her the file. She cried softly as she read his plan, but she was crying partly from relief. Her suspicions were right. She hadn't over-reacted. She wasn't crazy. He really was cheating. She was relieved because now she knew.

I've seen this mixture of sadness and relief before. Women put up with so much uncertainty. They squelch their misgivings, give their man the benefit of the doubt, re-interpret bad moments to be not so bad, and search out things they can do to help him feel better. But after a long enough time, the suspicions can no longer be ignored. They rise up like a creeping fog and completely consume the wife.

We copied the file and searched the office for any more information we might have missed. Even though we found a few more tidbits, I wasn't satisfied. I sensed we hadn't hit the jackpot. In the file there had been mention of a safe. "It has to be here," I thought. A cunning man like Alan wouldn't trust bank safety deposit boxes. So I kept opening drawers, checking corners. It was almost midnight when I found it, hidden in a wooden credenza behind Alan's desk. It was a sturdy steel safe with a combination lock, the kind of lock you don't pick.

I called Susan over and showed her the safe. She was so excited I thought she'd scream. "Can you blow it?" She asked.

I laughed and explained that blowing up a safe is only for the movies. An explosion big enough to pierce a double-layer steel safe is loud enough to alert police from three counties, send debris flying around, and damage half the stuff you're trying to get. Blowing up a safe is strictly for movie scriptwriters looking for special effects.

"We'll come back tomorrow night with a professional locksmith and open the safe ... quietly. He'll drill it out with a power drill. That's how we do things in real life."

Susan smiled sheepishly. We tidied up the office, putting the finishing touches on our visit. We erased every sign of our presence and made sure there were no papers in the copier. Then I called Steve on the walkie-talkie to check on the security guard's whereabouts. Steve told us to wait awhile. We settled in for the duration. Waiting is part of the "glamour" of being a private eye.

At 1:15 a.m., we got the "all clear" signal. I locked the office door and the outer door. We got past the security guard, jumped in the car, and drove away, carrying our bundle of incriminating evidence. The next night we were back with Eric, a haggard-looking professional locksmith in his 50's. Eric is something of a scholar on the subject of safes and loves to talk about them—their makes, styles, customers, and their strong and weak points.

Once we showed Eric the safe, it took him less than twenty minutes to open it. He didn't even want to look inside. Nervously accepting his $500 in cash for a good night's work, he made his departure as soon as Steve radioed us it was clear.

Susan and I opened the safe. "Oh, my God, I can't believe this!" she exclaimed. I had the same reaction. Inside was a real treasure. Stacks of hundred-dollar bills, enough to fill a briefcase: a small pile of negotiable bearer bonds, neatly banded in denominations of $50,000 and $100,000. Then there was the gold. Six gold bars gleamed at us, next to the hefty sack of South African Krugerrand gold coins. Rounding out the hoard were small black bags filled with emeralds, diamonds, opals, and rubies.

We stared. This is the stuff you see in the movies or in your dreams. I have never seen anything like it before or since. I stood there in a trance while fantasies of taking my wife on exotic vacations danced through my brain. Coming back to earth, I asked Susan if she wanted to count everything.

"Why?" She laughed gleefully. "It's all mine!"

I couldn't argue with that logic.

We carefully loaded everything in black nylon tote bags we had brought along. The hoard weighed at least 80 pounds. I offered to carry Susan's bag, but she wanted that honor for herself.

Steve told us we had just missed the guard's eleven o'clock pass, so we had a two-hour wait ahead of us before we could leave. We spent the time talking about Susan's plans. She would hide the loot in her own safety deposit box and prepare to file for divorce in a few months. After that, she wasn't sure—maybe spend some time with her family in Toronto … or travel.

"I can afford it now," she laughed.

We also spent some time perfecting our getaway. We had to make the visit look like a common burglary, so during the last twenty minutes Susan happily trashed files, upturned furniture, and generally created havoc in her husband's office. Right on time, Steve radioed that the coast was clear and we left as quietly as we had entered.

I wish I had been there Monday morning when Alan arrived for work. Instead of finding an orderly workplace, with secretaries dutifully taking calls and copiers humming, he found the chaos of overturned chairs, torn papers, spilled drawers, and a stunned staff.

I'm sure he immediately called the police, but he was in a bind only Susan and I could appreciate. If he reported the real extent of his loss, Susan would find out about it in the course of police questioning. To save the rest of his plan, he had to swallow the loss of cash, gold, and jewelry without a murmur.

Susan told me Alan was fuming that night when he got home. He asked her if she had been at the office. She'd answered coolly, "Why would I be at your office?"

Virtually beside himself, Alan told her about the burglary at his workplace—omitting, of course, any mention of the safe and its contents. Susan consoled him by saying, "Well, at least you didn't lose anything valuable!"

Desperate to recoup his losses, Alan accused his employees. Of course they denied any involvement. Now, in addition to everything else, he had alienated his staff.

Two days later Susan called to tell me his "little bank" had held more than $2 million and this was just a preliminary estimate! She hadn't had time to have the bonds and gems valued. Not bad for a guy pleading poverty! Best of all, he still didn't know about our break-in or our discovery of his incriminating file. That was a trump card almost as good as the loot in the safe.

Susan let Alan simmer for two more months, and then served him with divorce papers. In divorce court, he fought for every penny and calmly lied about his financial situation. Susan said the best moment of her life came when her lawyer, after making sure Alan had committed himself to a false declaration of his net worth, calmly introduced into evidence the file labeled "DIVORCE SUSAN."

After stammering out responses to the next few questions, Alan looked over at Susan, who smiled sweetly at him. As she said later, "He knew without a doubt that I knew what was in the file. He also knew that I had looted his office. I could see the color of his face turn from a normal color to bright red.

"You bitch! You bitch!"

"That's enough from you," said the judge.

"But your honor, she stole my money!"

"Money ... What money?" the judge asked.

"Forget it," Alan mumbled.

The information in the file made it abundantly clear to the court that this deceitful, ruthless man would have allowed his family to starve. No judge would be sympathetic to his settlement request. And the most satisfying part? By hiding the more than $2 million worth of cash, gold, bonds, and gems, he had dug his own grave. Unless he wanted to be indicted for perjury, he could not now ask for something that, according to him, didn't exist!

As we had expected, the judge awarded Susan most of the known community property, plus a guaranteed income from any corporation Alan owned now or might own in the future! That was the icing on the cake. Even if he earned a new fortune, he would have to split it with her.

Alan wound up with half of the house, which needed repairs that he now truly couldn't afford. The proceeds from the forced sale of his yacht and plane were split equally between Susan and Alan. The rest of his high-flying lifestyle evaporated in a puff of smoke. Everything he had planned for Susan—shock, carefully planned betrayal, and poverty—had happened to him. His lover probably took one look at Alan's new situation and lit out for greener pastures. Susan had her revenge—calm, cool, and collected.

A year later, we met again. Over drinks, Susan glowed with contentment and said how much happier she and the children were. They loved their new house, the kids' new school, and best of all, she loved her new freedom.

I felt pretty good about myself the rest of the day.

Susan was smarter than most women. She wanted revenge, but she also knew what was in her best interest. She got it all.

Here's what Susan did right: she let her rational mind overrule her emotions; she thought of her and her children's future when deciding what to do. She took the time to look for expert advice—and took it. She found out where the assets were before divorce proceedings started. That way she got her fair share—and then some. She also didn't tip her hand. After the break-in, Susan let her lawyer prepare divorce papers while she acted as if nothing out of the ordinary was going on. Did Susan do anything wrong? She shouldn't have worn high heels to a break-in.

Appendix A

□□□□□□□□□□□□□□□□□□□□□□□

The 40-Year Itch

Every woman should worry a little when her man turns 40. If a man is ever going to cheat, he's especially likely to do it around this time. Whenever a new client tells me she thinks her husband or boyfriend is cheating, I always ask, "Did he just turn 40?" They think I'm psychic!

I have asked men who have cheated on their wives, why they started at this time. They say they feel it's their last chance to turn back the clock. They think the future holds nothing but physical and sexual decline, and they want to stave it off. Taking stock of their lives, they question their successes, mull over their failures, and wonder about their relationships.

Some men feel they haven't had a great sex life with their wife for a long time, if ever. Of course, they don't think it's their own fault! An exciting illicit relationship seems like just the ticket. Getting a younger woman in bed makes a man feel young and virile again ... at least for a while.

Weight Loss

Many men (including me!) could stand to lose a few pounds. They might use the standard methods of exercise and diet, jogging, or giving up cheeseburgers for salads. However, it is noted that cheating is also an effective form of weight loss. A cheating man is trying to balance business, wife, and lover at the same time. That kind of effort eats up calories and interrupts mealtimes. Cheaters don't like to go to restaurants because they're too public, and precious stolen minutes with a lover aren't generally spent dining out. I've followed men who have lost as much as 50 lbs. during the course of an affair. I have never, ever seen a cheating man GAIN weight.

A man who is cheating doesn't even enjoy meals at home. If he has any conscience at all, facing the wife and children across the dinner table isn't easy. Family gatherings and other guilt-producing situations are even less palatable, and he tends to avoid them; that's another warning sign.

A New Look

A new wardrobe and suddenly improved personal hygiene are prime warning signs. A carpenter, plumber or repairman may suddenly start wearing new boots, a leather jacket or sports coat instead of the same old jeans and work shirt. A white-collar man may go the other way, replacing gray flannel suits with trendy casual clothes or cowboy gear. His clothes may look "younger." Suddenly, he's a fashion statement. The real giveaway is what he's wearing under those clothes, such as replacing the all-American white cotton briefs or boxers with expensive and colorful designer silk!

He may take steps to rejuvenate his appearance as much as possible. A graying man may tint his hair. He may grow a moustache and/or beard, or shave it off, to look more distinguished, virile, or to please the new lady in his life. A balding man may purchase a hairpiece, undergo surgical implants, or start combing over the remaining locks to hide the bald spot. He may trade his bifocals for contact lenses or sport fashionable eyewear frames.

Then there's the grooming fetish. When a man is getting dressed to meet his lover, he starts off with a shower and a careful shave. He may put on special cologne and take more time than usual to brush his hair so it looks just right. So if it seems like the old days when he knocked himself out to look sharp for a date—that may be exactly what he's doing!

Schedule Changes

The classic cover for a tryst is the excuse, "I have to work late tonight." Look for overall changes in work patterns. If a 9-to-5 man is suddenly putting in a lot of nights on the job, or if a graveyard-shift guy suddenly has to run errands during the day, take notice. Is he now so busy he doesn't have as much time for you? It takes a lot of time to maintain both a legitimate and an illegitimate relationship. He may be working harder ... but it ain't about the money!

Evasiveness

What happens when you ask him where he's been or why a bill hasn't been paid? He mumbles a vague answer, or becomes irritated by normal questions. He may be hiding something. If he's conducting a complicated affair (perhaps the other woman's husband is being deceived too), he has to keep track of a lot of things. For example, remembering what excuse he gave you last week and what story he gave his boss or secretary. He might be stalling for time by answering questions with questions while he tries to remember the multitude of alibis. He's paying dearly for not heeding Mark Twain's advice: "Always tell the truth. There's less to remember."

Money Problems

A cheating man may frivolously spend money on another woman, or he may carefully plot to squirrel away money and leave you penniless. Look for the following signs: bills aren't getting paid, he says business is bad, he becomes less communicative about finances, he doesn't want to indulge in your family's favorite pastimes, and 'cutting back' doesn't apply to him. Or he may do the opposite, suddenly showering you with gifts or extra treats, such as a day at the spa. He's quelling his guilt, keeping you busy, and hoping you'll be satisfied with this lavish attention.

The Health Club

A health club is a standard weapon in the cheater's arsenal. First, the co-ed clubs are an excellent source for scouting out potential lovers. Second, this is an ideal way to physically shape up, tone up and show off the new physique, and third on the list, he can go there to wash away the telltale evidence of a torrid rendezvous. This last item is crucial. He can't risk coming home trailing the scent of the other woman. A small stash of clean clothes will be stored at his workplace, gym, or in his car. The underwear he wore to the rendezvous gets tossed, the shirts are sent to the laundry. If he's cunning, he makes sure the clean shirts and underwear are the same brands worn when he left home. The health club is an excellent "home away from home" to shower and change before returning to you ... as if nothing has happened!

Of course, club membership may be perfectly innocent, so don't worry unless there are other danger signs.

Arguments

If a man is guilty of cheating, he wants to blame it on someone else. A classic way a cheating man justifies his affair is by trying to turn his innocent wife or girlfriend into an ogre. He picks fights by complaining about her cooking, her hair, and their child's behavior. Then, when the anticipated argument ensues, he feels justified in storming out of the house to meet the "understanding" lover.

Consciously or subconsciously, he wants to justify his need to have an affair. A man who starts one degrading petty argument after another often has plenty to hide, and is trying to transfer guilt from himself to his victim. All he needs is for her to react angrily. If she is too forgiving and he can't get a rise out of her, he may even become violent. Cheating can lead to physical abuse when the victim reacts with compassion or tears.

The Mysterious Telephone Calls

The telephone provides many clues: The wife comes home unexpectedly and her husband hurriedly hangs up the phone or his secretary stalls putting your call through. You may be surprised to learn that many telephone clues are not accidental at all; his lover is purposely sending you a signal! A cheating man usually thinks his new lover doesn't care about commitment. Because he's interested in just one thing (sex), he assumes that is her only interest too. Sometimes he's right. Maybe she has a marriage of her own she doesn't want to jeopardize, or perhaps she just wants a certain contained amount of contact.

But more times than not, a man is fooling himself when he thinks the other woman is satisfied with an illicit relationship. She may foster this impression, saying she doesn't mind his being married, doesn't want to have children of her own, is happy with things as they are. This is just what he wants to hear! In reality though, she really wants to break up the marriage and become Mrs. Cheater #2, #3 or #4.

For his part, the cheater usually tells his lover that he loves her, that his wife is boring, a shrew, hopeless in bed, that he has grown apart from her and will leave her soon. But he says he can't leave his wife until the kids have grown up, or a business deal has been completed, or his wife recovers from an illness. There are plenty of other stalling dodges, but these are the most popular ones. Two can play this game. Although his lover is lying, so is the cheater. The typical cheating man has no intention of leaving his wife. He still loves her, or is comfortable with her, or doesn't want to go through the upheaval of divorce. He wants it all ... the stable home life and the exciting extramarital affair, and for a while, he gets what he wants. But sooner or later, after a series of secret noontime trysts and hurried late-night embraces, the lover begins to want the cheater all to herself. If he's not doing anything to separate from his wife, the impatient lover decides to "help him along." She knows there's nothing to be gained by calling the wife directly because the wife would confront the man, he would confess and beg forgiveness, and he'd be furious with the tattling lover! So the lover gets the wife's attention by telephoning and hanging up just after an illicit meeting, trying to raise her suspicions. The lover's objective is to pressure the wife to accuse the cheater, forcing him to commit to the "innocent" lover. Sometimes this strategy works. Sometimes the wife comes to me first.

Another danger signal is a sudden desire on the man's part to control the home telephone. This isn't something you see with well-to-do cheaters. They usually have car phones and business phones available, and enough control over their work hours that they can slip away to make a call. You could say it is one of the fringe benefits of success. But for the majority of the population, cheaters can't call from work and it would attract unwanted attention if they ran out to a phone booth too often. So this man tries to call his lover frequently and may eventually, albeit recklessly, give her his home phone number, along with strict instructions as to how and when to call him. Most importantly, she will be instructed to hang up or ask for a phony name if anyone else answers the telephone. Take note if you receive calls asking, "Is Winston home?"

In any event, he will start watching over the phone like a hawk. He will try to answer the phone first. He may use the bedroom phone while you're in the kitchen or enjoying your favorite pastime. When you surprise him by walking into the bedroom, you'll notice that he's talking quietly and abruptly ends the call.

In summary, are you receiving a lot of "wrong number"calls or he rushes to beat you to the phone? Is he finding frequent reasons to go to the store or suddenly decides the dog needs to be walked? Any of these telltale signs may mean a lover is in the picture and he needs privacy to talk to her.

Remember, one sign alone isn't enough to make a diagnosis. Don't jump to conclusions because of a few wrong numbers.

Body of Evidence

Let's return to the lover who wants to sabotage her partner's marriage. What does she do? She leaves clues even the blindest wife would see. She's marking her territory! During sex, she digs her fingernails into his back and makes scratches. Her explanation (so flattering to his ego) is that he's such a red-hot lover; he drives her wild with passion. She may also secretly leave a smudge of lipstick behind his ear, or on his shirt, or the lingering scent of her perfume will embrace him for hours after they've parted. She might also leave telltale items like a lipstick case or compact in his car.

The average man doesn't suspect any of this. Men notice fine points in war and baseball, but are pretty dense about subtleties in relationships. The man's attention is focused on how gratifying the affair is. He is proud of himself and his sexuality and buys the line that the lover just can't control herself. "What a tiger he is!" He sees her as passionate and maybe a little forgetful. Just dispose of that one little item she mistakenly left behind. Surely, it won't happen again. But it does. The lover is planting a trail of clues for his wife to find, hoping the wife will notice and throw him out, ready to be picked up and caressed by the dutiful lover! One way to verify your suspicions is to sniff his clothing. It's not appealing, but it may be revealing. The other woman may use a distinctive perfume, hair spray, shampoo, deodorant, or other scented product. If your husband has been close to her, he is likely to pick up these telltale odors and he won't notice that he's reeking of her stale perfume.

The Car

For most of us, the car becomes our "mini home on wheels," and like any place where we reside, it tends to get a bit messy and cluttered. A man contemplating or indulging in an affair may take special care of his car, constantly having it washed and waxed, vacuuming the interior and cleaning the windows. Maybe he wants to make a good first impression. Maybe the actual sex takes place in the car. Cars are great mobile trysting places, where you can talk, neck, and go all the way, just as in the misspent days of his youth. So along with the cheater's personal appearance, the car's grooming is vastly improved too.

Your man may go a step further. Some cars are solid, dowdy, functional and sensible. Others are sleek, sexy and fast. If he rushes out to buy a new sports car or convertible, he may be hoping to recapture his youth and possibly a sleek, newer-model lover. When the cheater wants to dump the faithful station wagon for a high-powered Porsche or Corvette, he's telling you he wants to feel sexy and powerful.

Credit Card Statements

Using a credit card for the wrong purchase has caught more than a few cheaters. A man has to be truly stupid to buy flowers or rent hotel rooms and then let his wife see the bill. And there are some men who are that stupid! Or are they secretly hoping to be caught?

More commonly, cheating men will use a company card or pay cash for their lover's treats. Be on the lookout for odd receipts, especially in the car or his coat pockets. Men make this mistake often enough that it saves some wives the time and trouble of hiring an investigator

That Certain Smile

Here's a sign you might not expect—he is suddenly happy! A number of women have told me that what tipped them off to their husband's affair was that he suddenly started to come home in a good mood. One woman said, "I know something's up. He usually comes home and relaxes in front of the TV and mumbles, 'What's for dinner?' That's the only weekday evening conversation I've gotten out of him in 15 years. Now he comes home so happy and chatty, it makes me sick!"

Or maybe he buys you presents and begins remembering birthdays and anniversaries. This could be an attempt to assuage his guilt.

Appendix B

██████████████████████████

Signs and Portents

Men who cheat (and the women they cheat with) often give themselves away. They don't wear a scarlet letter like Hester Prynne, but an astute observer can easily pick up the signs.

- *Your man turns 40. (Not a sign, but an indicator).*

- *His appearance changes. He pays more attention to his personal hygiene ... like when he was dating you.*

- *He begins to pick petty arguments with you.*

- *You receive a flurry of mysterious phone calls.*

- *You detect scratches, lipstick smudges, or fragrances on his clothing or body.*

- *He cleans up the old car or gets a new one.*

- *Unexplained credit card purchases.*

- *His mood changes.*

- *He says he's working late but you don't believe it because he's never worked late before or he's never there when you call.*
- *He's lost weight.*
- *He joins a health club.*
- *He talks softly on the phone and hangs up when you enter the room.*
- *He buys a new wardrobe.*
- *He criticizes you or your manners.*
- *He keeps his e-mail password private.*

Appendix C

When Not to Be Suspicious

Even though I'm in the business of catching wayward spouses and "significant others," I don't want to sow suspicion where it shouldn't be. Sometimes apparent danger signs are actually innocent.

Schedule

Late nights "at work" may be absolutely genuine. A man may have a seasonal rush, a deadline on a big project, a staff shortage, or a co-worker out on sick leave. Is he a workaholic or is his ego is so bound up in his professional advancement that work is his mistress? (That may not be much of a consolation, I know.) Maybe he's a worrier, frightened about the economy, or he's a foresighted father saving for the kids' college education. Perhaps an old classmate just made a career triumph and your man feels pressured to keep up. In the most ironic twist of all, he may be planning something special for you.

Why does a man place such a high priority on work? The psychologists tell us that the main source of a man's self-worth is competence, the feeling that he is skillful and successful. So if he can't talk to his kids, he may avoid that horrible feeling of being ridiculed by the youngsters by staying at work. If his age-mates are getting ahead, he may be trying to catch up. Yes, sometimes the man really is at work ... actually working ... exactly like he says he is!

Weight Loss and Health Club

Television, newspapers and magazines deluge us with features about ways to improve our health, and weight loss is at the top of the list. Many men look around, see their friends dropping dead or undergoing heart surgery, and decide to take off the weight, just to be safe. Isn't this what you, his life-mate, really want? In addition to heart conditions, excess weight can contribute to a multitude of health problems. Could he be losing weight in order to live longer for you and your family?

Common Sense about Scents

Theoretically, there might be an innocent explanation for unusual scents on him or his clothes. He might have gotten too close to a pushy perfume demonstrator in a department store or stood in a crowded elevator next to someone who really doused herself. An unusual scent is not necessarily a smoking gun.

Mysterious Phone Calls

Is there anyone else in your house who might be playing pranks or who has mischievous friends? Elementary school kids often call each other while playing games. Teenagers may have bashful admirers too shy to speak. The cheater's "playmate" will do it more regularly and with precision.

Arguments

A husband's ill temper might stem from a legitimate cause, such as business troubles, a family member in need, or an undiagnosed medical problem.

Jumping to Conclusions

Weigh all the signs against the reality of your family life before jumping to conclusions.

Appendix D

Hiring A
Private Investigator

There are many instances when hiring a private eye is a must. For example, when you have a physical handicap that doesn't allow you to participate, or you have day-to-day commitments that just won't allow for the time it takes to conduct your own investigation. Fear of getting caught or being seen is one of the most common concerns for the do-it-yourselfer. Are you so despondent over the possible end of your relationship that you can't bring yourself to discover the truth on your own?

It's wise to shop around before hiring an investigator. It's important to know the investigator's area of expertise. How long has the investigator been in the business? Does the investigator specialize in surveillance, and especially as it relates to domestic matters? A phone call to the Department of Consumer Affairs in Sacramento will give you more information about the licensee. In states outside of California, the State Licensing Department usually handles Private Eye certificates and licenses.

About the Authors

Greg & Ann met in April 1973, when Ann was working as a legal secretary for a law firm in Walnut Creek, CA and Greg was working in high-tech electronics. At Lyon's Restaurant one April day. Greg fell madly in love with Ann from the moment he sighted her having lunch with a friend. With Greg's divorce nearly final, Greg proposed to Ann on his birthday, January 17th, 1974, and within three months the pair were wed. Ann's abilities with the printed word and Greg's oral communication skills were a perfect fit for a writing family. Greg talks, Ann writes. Greg has two children from his previous marriage, Wendy and Sean, and two children with Ann, Robert and Emily. The family also includes two dogs and three cats. In the nearly 30 years that Greg and Ann have been together, Greg and Ann have worked together as private eyes for seventeen of those years. Ann presently works at a high school in Walnut Creek, and on occasion she will put on her decoder ring and set out for another exciting investigation.

This book is based on true stories over a period of 25 years dealing with infidelity. The names and locales were changed to protect the privacy of our clients. Any similarities are coincidental. We do not condone violence in any form; these stories are not meant to inspire the readers to commit revenge on their partners. Doing so could result in serious injuries. This book was written to enable those in bad relationship to see that they are not alone nor are they losing their minds. There is always a tomorrow.

Contact Us

Clouthier Investigations
1630 N. Main St., Suite 200
Walnut Creek, CA 94596
E-Mail: clouthier@astound.net

Website

www.womansrevenge.com